"Why is it so easy for me to be deceived? Because he's clever. Shrewd. Scheming. Just a few of the Deceiver's descriptive attributes we realize in Jared C. Wilson's latest tome. Throughout *The Gospel According to Satan*, Jared enumerates the major ways the devil uses his cunning and calculating ways of luring us off the narrow road of God's grace. We will all do well to read this book and confront the lies we are being sold."

—KYLE IDLEMAN, SENIOR PASTOR OF SOUTHEAST CHRISTIAN
CHURCH AND AUTHOR OF *NOT A FAN* AND *DON'T GIVE UP*

"Satan sells poisonous lies that masquerade as liberating truths. Dare I say, some of his lies sound so good you might even want to believe them anyway. Jared Wilson wastes no words in this book that shines the light of God's Word into the darkest corners of the human heart. You'll wince with conviction, rejoice over truth, and be equipped to stand firm whenever Satan whispers, 'Did God really say…?'"

—COSTI W. HINN, PASTOR AND AUTHOR OF *GOD,*
GREED, AND THE (PROSPERITY) GOSPEL

"Jared Wilson is one of the most thought-provoking writers in the Christian world today, and *The Gospel According to Satan* is Exhibit A. Jared doesn't just describe the tantalizing falsehoods of our age, he exposes how they've slithered into our hearts. As you read this timely book, yes, you will confront lies you didn't even know you believed. But you will also encounter the gift of truth—which will set you free."

—MATT SMETHURST, MANAGING EDITOR AT THE GOSPEL
COALITION AND AUTHOR OF *BEFORE YOU OPEN YOUR BIBLE:*
NINE HEART POSTURES FOR APPROACHING GOD'S WORD

"We see the goodness of the gospel in fresh and vivid light when we see it against the backdrop of the alternative messages we so often slide into believing. Jared Wilson presents a unique, compelling, and even witty look at the devil's current greatest hits—lies we urgently need to unmask if we're to live in the fullness of God's truth in Christ."

—SAM ALLBERRY, SPEAKER FOR RAVI ZACHARIAS INTERNATIONAL
MINISTRIES AND AUTHOR OF *7 MYTHS ABOUT SINGLENESS*
AND *WHY DOES GOD CARE WHO I SLEEP WITH?*

"In his characteristic fashion, Wilson writes with accessible prose, pastoral insight, and refreshing honesty as he confronts the lies Satan tells us (and that we're all too prone to believing). Each chapter not only reveals the bondage that comes from buying into the enemy's schemes, but more importantly reveals the gospel's answers that bring true liberation. The book is so relevant to the struggles we all face that I heartily recommend it to as many as possible."

—ERICK SORENSEN, PASTOR OF EPIPHANY CHURCH
IN NEW YORK CITY, AUTHOR, AND COHOST OF THE *30*
MINUTES IN THE NEW TESTAMENT PODCAST

"More than a half century ago, J. I. Packer famously said that 'a half-truth masquerading as the whole truth becomes a complete untruth.' There is no more pressing need in our day than for us to get the gospel right. Satan would love for us to embrace an imitation gospel that ultimately keeps us far from the kingdom of God. Jared's book is a needed antidote to the imitation gospel poison that is being advanced in our day."

—BOB LEPINE, COHOST OF *FAMILYLIFE TODAY* AND
TEACHING PASTOR AT REDEEMER COMMUNITY CHURCH

"One of the joys and curses of our day and age is the frequency and diversity of messages that come across our paths. Whether an advertisement in our inbox, a soundbite on the radio, or a post or meme on social media, everywhere we turn it seems we are bombarded with voices. These messages inform us on everything from how to vote, where to travel, and what to buy. While most of us regularly dismiss this as background noise there arises at times the subtle temptation to buy into some ideas within popular culture without much thought. One common mistake that many of us make is that we fall for things that look and sound right, but upon further reflection aren't. In *The Gospel According to Satan*, author Jared Wilson helpfully examines several popular assertions from mainstream culture that sound innocuous and even inspired but when closely examined fall short of the truth. With wisdom, pastoral warmth, and biblical integrity, Wilson reflects on some of the common cultural maxims of our days and reveals not only their flaws, but more importantly how the grace of God shown in the gospel of Jesus provides the real solution to humanity's deepest longings. I found this book to a provide a clarion voice of truth in a world of confused clichés. Thank you, Jared."

—REV. DR. MALCOLM GILL, LECTURER AT SYDNEY
MISSIONARY & BIBLE COLLEGE, SYDNEY, AUSTRALIA

"If the devil's greatest trick was convincing the world he didn't exist, his second-greatest was convincing the world to believe lies that seem *almost* true enough to be true. This book exposes these sorta-kinda-not-really-truths for what they are and shows us why the gospel is better than the lies the devil is selling."

—AARON ARMSTRONG, BRAND MANAGER OF THE GOSPEL PROJECT
AND AUTHOR OF *EPIC: THE STORY THAT CHANGED THE WORLD*

"If Satan were to have his own Unholy Bible that he was the center of and unbelieving followers lived by, it would no doubt contain a book much like the book of Proverbs. This would be a whole book filled with godless and damning un-truisms like: 'God helps those who help themselves,' 'You only live once,' 'Live your truth,' 'Let go and let God,' among others. They would all be lethal—feigning the true Gospel but empty on the inside. In *The Gospel According to Satan*, Wilson exposes the fabricated wisdom and many false gospels of Satan and dismantles them with Scripture's most precious and powerful doctrines."

—SAM BIERIG, DEAN OF SPURGEON COLLEGE

THE GOSPEL
ACCORDING TO
• SATAN •

THE GOSPEL
ACCORDING TO
• SATAN •

EIGHT LIES
ABOUT GOD
THAT SOUND LIKE
THE TRUTH

JARED C. WILSON

NELSON
BOOKS
An Imprint of Thomas Nelson

Published in Nashville, Tennessee, by Nelson Books, an imprint of Thomas Nelson. Nelson Books and Thomas Nelson are registered trademarks of HarperCollins Christian Publishing, Inc.

Published in association with Don Gates of the literary agency, The Gates Group.

Thomas Nelson titles may be purchased in bulk for educational, business, fund-raising, or sales promotional use. For information, please e-mail SpecialMarkets@ThomasNelson.com.

Unless otherwise noted, Scripture quotations are taken from the Christian Standard Bible. Copyright © 2017 by Holman Bible Publishers. Used by permission. Christian Standard Bible®, and CSB® are federally registered trademarks of Holman Bible Publishers, all rights reserved.

Scripture quotations marked NASB are from the New American Standard Bible®. Copyright © 1960, 1962, 1963, 1968, 1971, 1972, 1973, 1975, 1977, 1995 by The Lockman Foundation. Used by permission. (www.Lockman.org)

Scripture quotations marked NIV are from the Holy Bible, New International Version®, NIV®. Copyright © 1973, 1978, 1984, 2011 by Biblica, Inc.® Used by permission of Zondervan. All rights reserved worldwide. www.Zondervan.com. The "NIV" and "New International Version" are trademarks registered in the United States Patent and Trademark Office by Biblica, Inc.®

Any Internet addresses, phone numbers, or company or product information printed in this book are offered as a resource and are not intended in any way to be or to imply an endorsement by Thomas Nelson, nor does Thomas Nelson vouch for the existence, content, or services of these sites, phone numbers, companies, or products beyond the life of this book.

ISBN 978-1-4002-1206-4 (eBook)
ISBN 978-1-4002-1204-0 (TP)

Library of Congress Control Number: 2019947733

Printed in the United States of America
HB 11.28.2023

This book is dedicated to the memory
of Richard Shawn Scott II.

CONTENTS

THE ANATOMY OF A LIE

Did God really say . . . ?
—THE SERPENT

BEFORE THERE WAS DEATH, THERE WAS THE LIE.

It begins as a question, a splinter of inquiry slipping smoothly under the skin of the mind. But it's not a question, really. It is a proposition wearing a mask. The question is a strange new idea, a smuggled roster of "alternative facts" holding out the prospect of curiosities sated, mysteries solved, even of enlightenments achieved.

The question goes like this: "Did God really say . . . ?"

It does not shock you. It does not immediately jar your religious sensibilities or theological knowledge. It arches an eyebrow, furrows a brow, twists up the corner of a mouth.

"Well, did he?"

Maybe we don't know. Maybe we think we know.

But the question has already begun its work. The splinter has already planted its bacterial doubt. The infection has begun.

Before there was death, there was the lie.

But before the lie, there was the Liar.

We assume he came from heaven, where the lies he told to himself required his expulsion. Having once enjoyed the splendid bliss of dwelling in the midst of the glory and holiness of the triune God, he bristled, begrudged. How it began, we don't know. Perhaps he began to sing the songs too falsely, too inwardly. Perhaps he conspired for what was not his.

In any event, the Liar began as one of God's heavenly host. He was an angel—still is, actually, but back then he was a good one. This was before he asked the questions that weren't really questions and before whatever light he carried was hurled from the celestial mountain down to the dust. He was thrown fast as lightning, so terrible was his betrayal of his Creator.

How long he stewed in the filth of his own imbecility and treason, we don't know. Was time then even a thing?

But later it was. God made it. He made all things. And he made all things good.

And there Satan thought he saw his opening again.

He didn't saunter into that garden. He got on his belly and crawled, to feign humility perhaps. In the dawn of precious creation, snakes didn't have the image we have of them today. No, that all started with *him*, with this. Before there was death, there was the lie.

Genesis 3:1 says the serpent was "cunning." He knew he could not bombard his quarry with outright heresy. He couldn't nag or cajole her. He could not appear as his true self, whatever that might look like: the anti-God, Antichrist, and anti-Spirit—a soul-sucking void of unrighteousness, stinking of rot and hell.

"Did God really say," he asked, "'You can't eat from any tree in the garden'?" (Gen. 3:1).

In the garden, the serpent planted the world's first seed of doubt.

> The woman said to the serpent, "We may eat the fruit from the trees in the garden. But about the fruit of the tree in the middle of the garden, God said, 'You must not eat it or touch it, or you will die.'" (Gen. 3:2–3)

Did she even know what "to die" means? She must have, or the Lord would not have promised it as a consequence. The man and woman both, enjoying the warmth of the gentle sun on their unashamed nakedness, the soft grass under their feet, the joys of unhurried and unbothered work and the sweetness of unhindered marital intimacy, and—best of all—personal communion with their beautiful Creator, would at least have understood that whatever "to die" meant, it was the reversal, the undoing, the erasing of all of that.

The world was full of possibilities. And here was one more: What if God was, in fact, *wrong*?

Was that possible? What if he didn't actually know what he claimed to know? What if, despite all the available evidence and in opposition to everything she'd ever experienced of his character, *God* was the one lying and not this character hissing seductively in her ear?

> "No! You will not die," the serpent said to the woman. "In fact, God knows that when you eat it your eyes will be opened and you will be like God, knowing good and evil." The

woman saw that the tree was good for food and delightful
to look at, and that it was desirable for obtaining wisdom.
(Gen. 3:4–6a)

It was that simple and that complex. The prospect of the lie
was a full-frontal assault on all of her senses, every point of won-
drous contact. Adam and Eve did not lack for food, and yet this
fruit looked "good for food," promising to satisfy in a way yet
undiscovered. The world was new and grand, and yet this fruit
was "delightful to look at," dazzling in a tantalizingly different
way. Adam and Eve had unfallen minds with an incredibly vast
capacity for learning, and yet this fruit "was desirable for obtaining wisdom," as if it held the key to the one locked door in their
imagination, the door into the one room they didn't even know
existed until the serpent shined his light on it.

I wonder what the fruit tasted like. Was it juicy and delicious?
Or was it maybe more bitter than they expected, a little thick,
like biting into an unripe peach? Maybe at the first bite they had
the first doubt of their choice—"What if this doesn't do what the
serpent said it would?"—but they kept eating, just in case. They're
just like us. Rather, we are just like them.

There is the epicenter of the mess you and I are in today. We
create our own craters of dysfunction and disease by our own disobedience, to be sure, but this is the point at which the contagion
at work within us entered the world. The garden of Eden, at the
precise moment Adam's perfect teeth broke the skin of that forbidden fruit, is Ground Zero. "Then the eyes of both of them were
opened, and they knew they were naked; so they sewed fig leaves
together and made coverings for themselves" (Gen. 3:7).

The repercussions are swift and vast. God calls them to account.

You can hear his footsteps in the garden. They are perhaps the footsteps of the pre-incarnate, uncreated Christ, seeking out his created siblings for their reckoning. The rest of Genesis 3 shows us that Adam and Eve are brought back out into the light to have their sin accounted for. Their sentence is pronounced, and it includes exile. They are cast out of the garden.

We've been trying to get back in ever since.

But you and I are not as clever as we think we are. We keep reasoning that the way back—the way to peace, fulfillment, wisdom—is the way that got Adam and Eve kicked out in the first place. We can't get in the same way we got out. But we try. And the serpent is still more than happy to oblige with his coaching. He is more cunning than we think he is.

See, the prospect of the fruit promised the three things—fulfillment, beauty, and enlightenment—that we have been chasing in every tree ever since. As Frederick Leahy has written, "The presuppositions of modern thought were introduced into Eden by Satan . . ."[1]

We live our lives in exile, but we play "garden" every day. We drink the mirage's sand and call it living water. We indulge our flesh and call it glory. We worship ourselves and call it living at the "next level."

Our hope is as it has always been—knowing God and living in communion with him—but we pretend that the divorce isn't real, that the disconnect is negligible. Or worse: we call the devil's lies the God's-honest truth.

That is what this book is about. Because most people can spot most lies coming. But what is it that made Adam and Eve so vulnerable to the serpent? What did he say, and how did he say it, that made it so compelling and so convincing? He was tempting them to disobey their Creator, yes, but he didn't just come out and say, "Disobey your Creator."

No, as we've seen, he promises fulfillment, beauty, and enlightenment. Similarly, the lies we believe today that erode our dependence on God and discredit our belief in the good news of his Son Jesus are not blatant. They are subtle. They make promises. They seem plausible. In Colossians 2:4, the apostle Paul warns Christians this way: "I am saying this so that no one will deceive you with arguments that sound reasonable."

Paul knew that unreasonable arguments won't hold much sway. It's the arguments that "sound reasonable," that sound truthful, that may in fact have some bit of truth mixed in, that so often keep us preoccupied. We're not looking to reject Jesus and shake our fist at God; we're just looking for a little more, a little better, a little greater.

Our enemy has now had centuries of practice at brand marketing. He will not show himself as he truly is. In 2 Corinthians 11, Paul is explaining the rot of heresy threatening the integrity of the church, the infiltration of false teachers who sound compelling and winsome and true, and he writes this:

> For such people are false apostles, deceitful workers, disguising themselves as apostles of Christ. And no wonder! For Satan disguises himself as an angel of light. So it is no great surprise if his servants also disguise themselves as servants of righteousness. (vv. 13–15a)

The correlation here between satanic deceit and religious respectability is vitally important, and it's one of the reasons for this book. The devil is adept at making sin look good. He knows if you see the reality of sin—and the reality of himself—you would be less inclined to follow him. Mike McKinley described the enemy's machinations like this:

> Think for a second what it would be like if Satan were to tell the truth when he tempted people? Could you picture what that would look like? Imagine if Satan tried to tempt us honestly; it might go something like this:
>
> SATAN: You should cheat on your wife with that good-looking girl in the office.
> PERSON: I don't think so. It's wrong, and it would hurt my wife.
> SATAN: Fair enough; you make a good point. But look, I've run a cost-benefit analysis for you. Here's what I've come up with:
>
> Benefits:
> 1. A few moments of physical (if perhaps awkward) pleasure.
>
> Costs:
> 1. Disobedience to God.
> 2. Erode your communion with God.
> 3. Ruin, or possibly even end, your marriage.
> 4. Humiliate your wife.
> 5. Mess up your kids' lives.
> 6. Public humiliation and exposure.
> 7. Might cost you your job.
> 8. Might mess up your coworker's life.
> 9. Diseases?

10. Unwanted pregnancy?
11. Dishonor and disgrace on your church.
12. Wreck your witness to others.

PERSON: Yeah, wow. Umm . . . no, thanks.[2]

Of course, the first trick the devil tries to pull is getting you to disbelieve in his existence in the first place. But if he can't manage that, he will want you to think you can always see him coming from a mile away. McKinley's humorous illustration shows how silly such a notion would be. No, the best trick of the devil is getting you to think his ideas aren't just yours, but even *God's*.

So he creates his own "gospel," a perversion of the real one. It sounds like good news because it appears to answer questions we've always had, satisfy desires we've always felt, solve mysteries we've always pondered. If he can give his lies the ring of truth, so much the better.

If I were making a list of benefits like the one Mike McKinley imagines, only this time using the devil's actual logic, it might look more like this:

1. Experience the excitement of new romance.
2. Get the kind of satisfaction my wife isn't willing to give or interested in giving anymore.
3. Find someone who listens to me and actually understands.
4. Relieve this stress and boredom.
5. Feel attractive and desired.
6. Feel loved.

Those are the lines we follow when we ponder affairs. We give an inch at a time, compromise after compromise, not in the explicit interest of disobeying God and dishonoring our marriage vows, but in the interest of fulfillment, beauty, and enlightenment. Sin makes an emotional kind of sense to us that defies biblical reason, and the devil is more than happy to help us with that too. After all, God forgives anything, right?

So this is why Satan comes to us as an angel of light, promising illumination and enlightenment. But in the end, he only delivers us into darkness and despair.

It's important, then, to have our eyes open to this deception. How is it that so many modern promises sound true but in the end lead to our deception, or even our destruction? A long, long time ago, the English Puritan Thomas Brooks wrote:

> Now the best way to deliver poor souls from being deluded and destroyed by these messengers of Satan is, to discover them in their colours, that so, being known, poor souls may shun them, and fly from them as from hell itself.[3]

In other words, the best thing to do is to expose the lies, examine how they work, explore why they're so compelling, and explain how to overcome them with the truth. We must "discover them in their colours." In the pages ahead we will look at the following claims, each of which enjoys a degree of popularity today—some even within our own churches—and we're going to see why they're not all they're cracked up to be.

In the first chapter, we'll examine the idea that "God just wants you to be happy." Is this really true? Is this all God wants?

What if God isn't as interested in our happiness as he is in other things? And what if that's actually good news?

"You only live once." Not just a now-outdated hashtag or instantly regrettable tattoo, the spirit of this claim is as old as the hills. You may think YOLO is lame, but you are nevertheless tempted to abide by it every single day, so in the second chapter, we'll give some attention to the radical promise (and deficiency) of living life by the mantra of *carpe diem*.

In the third chapter, we will take a look at the subtle Oprah-ization of the Christian faith. We see it in every self-absolving apology and sheepish declaration of self-empowerment, and we're beginning to see it among professing Christians too. What's wrong with the idea that "you need to live your truth"?

It is similar to the universal lie covered in the fourth chapter: "Your feelings are reality." This is the lie we're afraid is true. This is the lie so many of us don't want to believe in. And yet we do. This is a particularly pernicious deception in the satanic arsenal, and we will go hard at it. This chapter could very well save your life.

The fifth chapter in some ways examines the heart of the original serpentine question. When Satan asked Eve, "Did God really say . . . ?" he was intimating that God is holding out on us. This is our fear. And thus our essential belief whenever we choose sin over obedience is the lie that "your life is what you make it."

In the sixth chapter, we will look at a phrase that has plagued the church in the modern age, one you still find in social media memes and comments, ladled out like chicken soup for the superficial soul. "You need to 'let go and let God.'" There is a kernel of truth in this lie, which is what makes it so easily dispensed and so deceptively destructive. Playing on our religious sensibilities, this lie appeals in a way the others do not.

While the sixth chapter examines a lie that plays on our religious sensibilities, the seventh examines one that plays on our theological sensibilities by way of our emotions. You may not have heard this lie reach your church quite yet, but it is becoming fashionable in modern evangelicalism, and it's important we confront it head-on ahead of time: "The cross is not about wrath." The arguments seem sound, but the result is an attempt at rescuing God from the Bible. The cross is about more than wrath, of course, but it's not about less. And this is important, especially if you want the kind of relationship with Jesus that *avoids* wrath.

The final lie exposes the mother of all religious clichés: "God helps those who help themselves." That's the common wording, though the message underneath the cliché is more accurately phrased, "God saves those who help themselves." That's not how the devil puts it, but that's what we end up believing—which makes him happy. We close with the confronting of this lie because it will bring us full circle, back to that original garden and then to another garden much later on, where the lie was exposed and ultimately killed.

When we're done exploring the ins and outs of all these temptations and deceptions, we'll take a more open-eyed look at how we get altogether out of the exile that makes these lies so doggone believable. How do we spot them coming? How do we fight the enemy who delivers them? And how do we put a knife in the body of lies for good? In our concluding chapter, we'll perform the Autopsy of the Lie that will prove helpful in our fight to embrace the truth.

For now, however, it's enough to remember the anatomy of

the lie: fulfillment, beauty, and enlightenment. Who wouldn't want those things?

The answer is, nobody. Which is why we so often find Satan's whispers so sweet.

Well, let me tell you the bitter truth. And the better.

GOD JUST WANTS
YOU TO BE HAPPY

*An ever increasing craving for an ever
diminishing pleasure is the formula.*

—C. S. LEWIS, *THE SCREWTAPE LETTERS*

I JUST DON'T UNDERSTAND WHY GOD WOULD MAKE
me this way only to tell me I can't be happy."

Gretchen* sat stiffly in the chair across from me, hands
cradling her iced latte. She didn't look nervous or confused. If
anything, she looked *decided*. This was clearly something she

---

* Gretchen is a composite of numerous persons—both male and female—I've
had this conversation with over my last decade of ministry. The conversation I'm
reconstructing here is a paraphrase representative of the exchange I've had with
each of them.

had thought about for a long time, and in a way, she was meeting with me not for counsel or even approval but to make an announcement.

I have been privy to numerous such announcements—most much less decided than Gretchen's, usually more inquisitive, more searching, more desperate for an answer. And I always wonder, why me?

I assume they come to me because in the minds of some, because of my vocation, I am representative of God. In an odd way, I sometimes think these meetings are requested with me because, as a minister, I very much serve as a stand-in for the God who, in my inquisitors' minds, isn't exactly talking back. They've prayed and agonized and wrestled, and they're not getting an answer—or at least, they're not getting the answer they want. Talking to me becomes a way to flesh out what seems so indecisive in their imagination.

Gretchen said she'd been attracted to women as long as she could remember. It wasn't anything she sought out. She said she wasn't molested, wasn't exposed to pornography. She'd had loving parents who by all indications had done their best. She wasn't necessarily sexually interested in women, she said, but she was definitely not attracted to men. Her story seems more and more common these days. "When all the girls started getting interested in boys," she said, "I found myself wanting to be more 'one of the boys.' And when all the girls wanted to date boys, I kind of played along, but I never felt anything. Only with girls did I ever feel a spark or want to be held or want to have long conversations. I feel like I could be really happy with one woman forever. This isn't something I chose. I was born this way."

I set that claim aside. As far as I can tell, it's neither here nor there. Some of us are born with certain attractions and some of us have those attractions cultivated in us through circumstances and environments. I'm not an expert on which applies to whom. And from my perspective, it's beside the point.

"Why are you telling me this?" I asked her. I ask this of everyone who tells me what Gretchen was telling me, though not always in the same way. They never say, "Because you represent God," though as I said, I think that's a huge part of it. They always say something like this: "Because you seem like someone who would understand."

I don't know why I give off this vibe, and to some extent, I'm sort of afraid of it. When I first assumed the pastorate of my previous church, one woman in the town suddenly resumed her church attendance. She was notoriously liberal (and I don't mean that as an epithet). Eventually, when someone got around to asking her why she was attending church again, she said it was because she assumed the new pastor was "open and affirming," by which she meant "open to full participation in the life of the church by practicing homosexuals and affirming of their orientation and lifestyle."

She was wrong, of course, and it didn't take her long to figure out from my preaching that I was just as "narrow-minded" as the "fundamentalists" who hired me—meaning, we all affirmed the traditional viewpoint of the Bible's prohibition of homosexuality— but I was curious why she had made this assumption about me. Had I said something that could be misinterpreted?

When I met face to face with that woman, she said she had made that assumption first because I was young, and she assumed that young Christians were more progressive than older Christians (which is generally true, actually). But she also assumed it because

I talked about grace a lot and had a comforting demeanor in the pulpit. I talked about sin a lot too—you actually can't talk about grace biblically without talking about sin—but I had talked about a bunch of other sins, mostly found among religious people, before I had talked about the sin of homosexuality, and in the interim her assumption was born.

Gretchen knew my position on homosexuality. She had heard me teach on the subject before. She had heard me say all the things biblically shaped preachers ought to say: homosexuality is a sin that offends the holy God, but God forgives and saves repentant gay folks just as well as straight, and that there is no sin too difficult for him. She'd heard me say that the church had failed young men and women who struggled with same-sex attraction by labeling that sin in particular as somehow worse or more culturally heinous than any others, and by failing to be merciful to those who doubt and gentle with those who need restoration. She'd heard me challenge the church to stop treating some people and certain sins as more acceptable than others, more redeemable than others. She'd in fact heard me invite anyone who struggled with same-sex attraction to trust their struggles to Jesus, same as anyone else, to repent and believe and find their peace in him.

She'd heard all of that and more, and she'd found it wanting.

But like that erstwhile churchgoer, Gretchen knew I was a big proponent of grace. And she thought if she couldn't put that to the test with me, she might not be able to put it to the test with anyone.

She had grown up hearing that homosexuality was a sin, and she could see that the Bible seemed to plainly say the same. And yet it didn't seem the same as other sins that appeared to be much more a matter of doing or not doing. Most things the Bible calls sin are matters of choice. You do them or you don't do them. You start doing them or you stop doing them. They didn't appear to her to be matters of the heart.

"I didn't choose this," she said. "It is a part of me. It *is* me."

In her mind, and in the minds of so many others, her sexual orientation was part of her identity, her "wiring." She hadn't chosen to be gay, she reasoned, any more than I had chosen to be straight. "Imagine if God forbid you from being straight," she said.

I thought to myself, *Well, there are certain ways of being "straight" that God does forbid*. But I didn't say that. Instead, I said, "First, thank you for sharing this with me. It tells me that for some reason you trust me. Second, though, I have to tell you that I don't think you're understanding grace in a way that's exactly biblical."

I tried to put it as gently and yet as clearly as I could, but it didn't quite land.

"I figured you'd say that," she said. "But you don't really know what this feels like."

"No, you're right. I don't know what this specific thing feels like. But I'm not a stranger to feeling like something is embedded in my bones, that there's a desire that I wish I could be rid of but for whatever reason God won't take away, and wondering what in the world I do with how it seems like I was made to be."

"What do you mean?"

"I mean, I can't speak with authenticity to being attracted to the same sex, but I can speak with experience to wondering why God would allow desires in me that he didn't want me to fulfill. Why would God make me this way only to keep me from being happy? I *do* understand that feeling."

And chances are, dear reader, you do too. Maybe you don't struggle with same-sex attraction, or maybe you do, but the idea that there are longings both innate to us and forbidden from us is a spiritual conundrum faced by everyone. Nearly every heterosexual Christian male I know has had to routinely mortify a lust for women that feels natural, instinctual. There are sins like gluttony and worry that seem to arise from the fabric of our very nature. And they do. Because our fallen nature will always haunt us this side of Christ's return.

But doesn't God want us to be happy?

Well . . . it's complicated. It's actually as complicated as we are.

When the serpent slithered up to Eve in the garden, what he was tempting her with did not fall far outside of her design. Fulfillment. Beauty. Enlightenment. These are all things God had created her to want. Indeed, Adam and Eve had been created with an endless capacity for fulfillment, beauty, and enlightenment, provided they were oriented in the right direction. Her grasp for them in a way strictly forbidden was the problem, but her capacity for them was part of her design.

Now, before I go too far, I want to reiterate that I do not believe homosexuality is part of God's design for human beings. Like all sexual sin, including sinful desires experienced heterosexually (or solosexually), homosexuality is a consequence of the fall, in essence a departure from God's good design for men and women and their experience of sexuality. And this is true of all sexual sin—that is, the expression of sexuality in ways explicitly forbidden by the Bible. All sexual immorality is a corruption of something good, of even *desires* that are essentially good. These include things like relational intimacy and the experience of true love. We were made to know and be known. We were made to experience love. Therefore, these desires are not sins, even if the ways we feel wired to satisfy them so often are. This isn't a distinctly "gay" phenomenon. This side of the fall, it's just being human.

And this is why I told Gretchen she wasn't seeing the whole picture in relation to grace. Most of the time, we think of sin like she did—things you do or don't do. And then grace is what lets you off the hook when you get it wrong. But sin is much bigger than that. And so is grace.

Sin in fact is very much about how we're wired. Sinful actions are simply the outward expressions of our sinful nature. This is one reason why Jesus in his famous Sermon on the Mount began reframing the place of sin from outward behavior to inner character. He was not saying that committing physical adultery is no big deal; instead, he was saying that any of us can be just as guilty of sexual sin as the physical adulterer, because the sinful disorder begins in our inner selves. The same goes for his correlation between murder and anger.

Sin isn't purely about the malfunction; it's essentially about the faulty wiring.

In that regard, grace is not simply about pardoning sinful behavior; it's also about rewiring the sinners themselves. The grace the Bible talks about is power not just for justification but also for transformation.

To get a better vision of how big God's grace really is, however, we have to see the lie that leads us astray for what it is. And though "God just wants me to be happy" seems pretty simple and straightforward, it's a compelling lie for a fairly complex reason. It has all the longing of the human soul inside of it. So we are up against the world here. And we have to first be careful in understanding why this claim is not true and, second, be careful in the truth we use to counteract it.

There are actually two lies related to God and happiness that operate as a kind of yin and yang in the Christian imagination. We'll take them one at a time.

THE FIRST SIDE OF THE LIE: GOD JUST WANTS YOU TO BE HAPPY

You don't have to be gay to believe the meeting of your romantic and sexual desires will finally make you happy. I know, because this has been my struggle for most of my life. I remember lying awake at night in my teenage bedroom, staring at the ceiling, fighting tooth and nail against the lust that seemed to come as natural as breathing, and praying to God to give me a girlfriend. If I only had a girl I could love and be loved by, I wouldn't struggle so much with the sin in my mind.

Of course, I was fooling myself. I was imagining that all my misplaced desires were really about romantic love, that if I had someone to love who would love me back, all my angst would go quietly away. When we're spiritually sober, we know it doesn't work that way.

In the biblical book of Ecclesiastes, King Solomon is an old man looking back on his youth and all the time he wasted trying to fulfill desires that were too big to be contained. He had everything anybody could ever want. He imagined having all the sex he could desire would solve the ache in his heart. Didn't work. He imagined having all the natural beauty his eyes could take in would do the trick. Didn't work. He imagined all the money, all the mansions, all the majesty of power and wisdom would finally calm the storm in his soul. It didn't work.

Why? Because his heart had an eternal gap in it (Eccl. 3:11), and none of those things was eternal.

Incidentally, this is why your dietary "cheat day" or a night out drinking doesn't really relieve the stress built up by the workweek. It's why the porn you looked at last night only left you feeling ashamed, not satisfied. And it's why even the perfectly adequate spouse you either desire or actually have hasn't totally made you at ease with the problem of you.

I'm in my forties now, safely removed from the teenage years but not from all my teenage dumbness. I still think, *If I only had _____, I'd finally be happy.* What fills in the blank is a little different depending on my season of life or even the circumstances of my day, but I repeat the same error over and over. I think something temporary will solve something eternal.

This is perhaps Satan's greatest hit. If he can get our eyes lowered to ground level in search of fulfillment, beauty, and enlightenment, he's already most of the way to getting us to disobey. This is a go-to move for him, because it's already the built-in bent of our hearts. Because of the sin nature we are all born with, our eyes naturally drift downward to ourselves and the things around us. In fact, it takes supernatural help to lift our gaze to behold the ultimate fulfillment, beauty, and enlightenment of the glory of Christ. In a strange way, looking to God goes against our grain, so all the devil really needs to do is pet us. We like a good petting.

The search for happiness is probably the most universal experience for all people throughout all time. There is a reason, for instance, the evangelistic tract "The Four Spiritual Laws," famous since 1952, contains the promise "God loves you and has a wonderful plan for your life" instead of "God loves you and has a difficult plan for your life." The difficult part we already know. It's the wonderful part we *want*.

So when we hear the claim "God just wants you to be happy," it feels right.

There is a logic in the claim that God just wants us to be happy that is hard to dismantle. Like my friend Gretchen said, it's hardly a matter of doing or not doing. It's really a matter of being or not being. And we can trace the logic back up to our conception of God himself.

God made us. And God made us with the capacity for happiness. And he made us with unique interests, specific temperaments, and strong desires. What kind of God would want us to suppress those things? Why would he tease us that way?

God is good, isn't he? So why would a good God want us to be unhappy, living so untrue to ourselves?

If you recall, this is the tactic Satan took in the garden with Eve. In so many words, he said, "Look, why would God make you with the capacity for God-ness yourself and then keep you from it? Why not become like him?" In a way, she didn't even know what she was missing until the serpent told her she was missing out.

"You can do this," he implies. "So why wouldn't you?"

It's easy to locate the belief in this lie solely in the world of hedonistic pleasure. Most of us can look at the sex addict, the greedy money-grubber, the power-hungry abuser, or the gluttonous pleasure-hound and easily spot the counterfeit happiness, even when they themselves seem so blind to their own perversions. But it's the ordinary melancholy that gets most of us. You and I aren't perverted pleasure-cruisers. Right?

Well, maybe not. But we're on a parallel track every time we assume that if we're not happy, we are being robbed. Because, just like those gross perverts *out there*, we are bent toward our own happiness as the ultimate goal in life.

The hard truth is, God doesn't just want us to be happy.

GOD'S FIRST PRIORITY IN YOUR LIFE

"Just do good for your own self. Do good because God wants you to be happy."[1]

Thus spake Victoria Osteen from the stage of Houston's Lakewood Church in a now-deleted video that made a bit of a viral splash in 2014. Standing next to her husband and co-pastor, Joel, perhaps the world's most renowned proponent of self-help religion, what Mrs. Osteen said had a ring of truth to it. And it sure sounded good. "When we obey God," she said, "we're not doing it for God. . . . We're doing it for ourselves. Because God takes pleasure when we're happy. That's the thing that gives him the greatest joy."

It's quite a bold claim. But is it true?

As with most things, context is everything. And in a religious context in which sin is rarely if ever mentioned (much less rebuked), the cross of Christ seems more a bug than a feature. The prevailing message is "live your best life now," "become a better you," and "think better, live better," but the answer is no: God's greatest pleasure isn't our happiness. The Osteens and a handful of other prosperity gospel preachers have made this message their stock and trade. It is self-actualization masquerading as Christianity, and it resembles the spirituality of the New Age more than the spirituality of the Bible.

Why? Because God's priority in the Scriptures does not at all seem to be our happiness—at least, not so far as the Osteens of the world position it, in terms of health, wealth, and personal success.

What, then, is God's main priority for us? I mean, what in the world is he doing with us? You ever wonder that?

Before I answer that question, let me set up my answer with a brief survey of real life. Ready?

You and I come into this world through a very painful process for our mothers. Even if they've had the benefit of an epidural or other pain-relieving methods for childbirth. The time of pregnancy is hard. The giving birth is hard. And then we pop out, usually crying. We're sometimes happy as children but very often not. Then we grow up, and we get better about managing our emotions and rationalizing our unmet expectations—for the most part—but life is still hard. When we're little kids we think being teenagers will be awesome. Then we become teenagers and we wish we were adults. Then we're adults and we realize how much we miss being little kids.

Every stage of life contains tests of all kinds. Every stage of life brings new challenges, fresh hurts, unrealized dreams, and overwhelming fears. Then we get old, and everything starts hurting and falling apart. Then we die. As Job says, "Anyone born of woman is short of days and full of trouble" (Job 14:1). In other words, "Life stinks, then you die." (Don't ever let anybody say the Bible doesn't shoot straight.) You won't ever catch the prosperity gospelist preaching that!

Now, if we're lucky, sometime in the midst of all that trouble we take long walks on the beach, stare at sunrises and sunsets, go to the zoo, watch our kids play in the yard, laugh with friends over a board game or around a campfire, listen to Grandma sing a hymn while she makes cookies, hold hands with our spouse while watching a movie, get hugged and kissed a whole bunch, hear Handel's *Messiah*, see snow falling on a quiet Christmas morning, and experience a million other pleasures besides. We sometimes think those are all the things that make life worth living.

Which is why sometimes we don't think life is worth living, when we don't get enough, or any, of those things. The pains seem to outnumber the pleasures. Or even if we don't quite get to that kind of despair, we still from time to time beat against the hurt in our hearts that no earthly pleasure seems to console. We get sick—or worse, a loved one does. We mess up, sometimes in very big ways that hold no promise of being rectified. People insult us, betray us, or just change into other kinds of people we don't want to be friends with. Sometimes that person is our spouse or our child or our parent or our pastor. We lose jobs, we lose health, we lose vision. We go to doctors, to therapists, to life coaches. We go to church.

Sometimes the hurt isn't anything we can put our finger on. It's just there, weighing us down and hanging all around. It's a shadow hanging over us or a darkness buried deep inside of us.

If you believe in the biblical God—which is to say, the one Creator who is sovereign over all—somehow your version of his take on happiness has to accommodate for these realities.

The hurt is one reason why so many people reject the idea of God. They do not see how one who is all-loving and all-controlling could allow such pain and hardship in the world. He's either not all-loving or not all-controlling, they reason. And that makes perfect sense—*if* God's main priority for us is happiness.

When God summoned the apostle Paul into lifetime service in the cause of Christ, he puts it this way to Ananias: "I will show him how much he must suffer for my name" (Acts 9:16).

Later, Paul recounts his missionary adventures like this:

> Five times I received the forty lashes minus one from the Jews. Three times I was beaten with rods. Once I received a stoning. Three times I was shipwrecked. I have spent a night and a day in the open sea. On frequent journeys, I faced dangers from rivers, dangers from robbers, dangers from my own people, dangers from Gentiles, dangers in the city, dangers in the wilderness, dangers at sea, and dangers among false brothers; toil and hardship, many sleepless nights, hunger and thirst, often without food, cold, and without clothing. Not to mention other things, there is the daily pressure on me: my concern for all the churches. (2 Cor. 11:24–28)

If this is the biblical reality for those who pursue God like the apostle Paul, what hope do the rest of us "normal" people have?

I mean, if God just wanted us to be happy, he wouldn't have responded to Adam and Eve's rebellion with a curse (Gen. 3:13–19), would he?

So happiness must not be God's main priority for us. If it is, he's not very good at being God. Otherwise, life would simply consist of one pleasure after another.

Now that we've been reminded of reality, we come back to the question: What, then, is God's main priority for us? The answer is all over the scriptures. A sampling:

- "Abram believed the LORD, and he credited it to him as righteousness." —Genesis 15:6
- "Be my holy people."—Exodus 22:31

- "For I am the LORD your God, so you must consecrate yourselves and be holy because I am holy."—Leviticus 11:44
- "This way you will remember and obey all my commands and be holy to your God."—Numbers 15:40
- "We will be satisfied with the goodness of your house, the holiness of your temple."—Psalm 65:4
- "There is life in the path of righteousness, and in its path there is no death."—Proverbs 12:28
- "I will honor the holiness of my great name. . . . The nations will know that I am the LORD—this is the declaration of the LORD GOD—when I demonstrate my holiness through you in their sight."—Ezekiel 36:23
- "Blessed are those who hunger and thirst for righteousness, for they will be filled."—Matthew 5:6
- "But seek first the kingdom of God and his righteousness, and all these things will be provided for you."—Matthew 6:33
- "Since by the one man's trespass, death reigned through that one man, how much more will those who receive the overflow of grace and the gift of righteousness reign in life through the one man, Jesus Christ."—Romans 5:17
- "For he chose us in him, before the foundation of the world, to be holy and blameless in love before him." —Ephesians 1:4
- "Flee from youthful passions, and pursue righteousness."—2 Timothy 2:22
- "Pursue peace with everyone, and holiness—without it no one will see the Lord."—Hebrews 12:14
- "But as the one who called you is holy, you also are

to be holy . . . ; for it is written, Be holy, because I am holy."—1 Peter 1:15–16

- "Let the righteous go on in righteousness; let the holy still be holy."—Revelation 22:11

There are many more examples besides. But the bottom line is this: the through-line of the scriptures is that God has prioritized his own glory—over and over, we see how everything he says and does is to make his glory known, for his own "namesake"—and this means that his ultimate concern for us is that we be holy.

Now, holiness does not exclude happiness. They are not set against each other, as if to be holy necessitates being unhappy. Nor do we have any biblical basis from which to conclude that God is somehow happy that we are unhappy. I will say more about how happiness and holiness work together in a moment, but for now it is enough to see that *as a matter of priority*, God is much more concerned that we be holy than that we be happy.

Think of the ancient sufferer Job in the Bible. This man lost everything good in his life—his children, his livelihood, his possessions, and even his health. Sitting in a heap of ashes, scraping boils off his skin while his wife nags and his friends accuse and the devil afflicts, Job was most certainly not happy. And the emphasis of the entire book of Job is not that Job should look on the bright side of things. He could see none. The emphasis was not that he should think positively or put on a happy face or fake it till he could make it. No, the emphasis from God's perspective was that Job should know the glorious grandeur of the holiness of God and that Job himself should be holy too (Job 1:22).

This is important for the person who believes in the God of the Bible, because it means that while happiness may come and go depending on the circumstances of life or the disposition of our own temperament, holiness is always at hand. We can be holy even when we're not happy, and vice versa.

To be holy is to be "set apart," to pursue submission to God that reflects his existence and his character and that—this is important—more reflects the character of who we were created to be, the us whom we were before we believed the satanic lie that made us unholy.

This is what makes the half-truth, "God just wants you to be happy," so dangerous: The devil would be perfectly satisfied if we were perfectly satisfied apart from the holiness of God. He will do whatever it takes to get us interested ultimately in our own happiness. He doesn't care how we feel, so long as we're unrighteous. The devil would love for you to be perfectly happy, so long as you are not holy. He knows happily unholy people rob glory from God and go happily to hell.

So no, Victoria Osteen is not totally right when she says we ought to do good for ourselves instead of for God, because God's chief concern is not our pleasure but our holiness.

But neither is Osteen totally wrong.

THE OTHER SIDE OF THE LIE: GOD DOESN'T CARE IF YOU'RE HAPPY

As I said previously, there are actually two lies related to God and happiness that operate as a kind of yin and yang in the Christian imagination. The first is that "God just wants us to be happy." The problem with that lie is the word *just*. God's priority is not our happiness but our holiness. And yet, God is not disinterested in our

THE GOSPEL ACCORDING TO SATAN

happiness. So the other side of the lie is the opposite extreme: "God doesn't care if you're happy."

Those reacting to that lie were likely the most eager to believe Victoria Osteen's half-truth. And to be clear, what she said about obeying God not for him but primarily for us—that he's happy when we're happy—in context, is dead wrong and spiritually dangerous. She's derailed and in the ditch. But the right track is in eyesight.

Osteen is not *totally* wrong, because walking with God is a—let the reader understand—*happy* thing. It's a different kind of happy, to be sure. But it's a happy thing nonetheless. Not happy-go-lucky. Not happy in moments or gifts. But happy in the Sovereign, in the Giver. The eighteenth-century Anglican preacher George Whitefield explained:

> As it is an honorable, so it is a pleasing thing, to walk with God. The wisest of men has told us, that "wisdom's ways are ways of pleasantness, and all her paths peace." And I remember pious Mr. Henry, when he was about to expire, said to a friend, "You have heard many men's dying words, and these are mine: A life spent in communion with God, is the pleasantest life in the world." I am sure I can set to my seal that this is true. Indeed, I have been listed under Jesus' banner only for a few years; but I have enjoyed more solid pleasure in one moment's communion with my God, than I should or could have enjoyed in the ways of sin, though I had continued to have gone on in them for thousands of years.[2]

Whitefield, in his inimitable way, is helping us to remember the biblical truth that holiness and happiness are not opposed to each other but often go hand in hand. In fact, God is not opposed to our happiness; he only wishes that we find our ultimate happiness *in him*.

Reflecting on Mrs. Osteen's unfortunate mangling of priorities, Ligon Duncan nevertheless reminds us of something historic Christians, in contrast to many today, have believed about the pursuit of holiness:

> [O]ur chief and highest purpose, goal and end in life is God's glory. That is what we live for. Whereas many of our contemporaries think that God is the chief means to our highest end (happiness), [we] do not believe that God is a means to an end, he is The End. He is the reason and aspiration for which we exist. There is no ultimate happiness and satisfaction and fulfillment and joy apart from him.[3]

In a 2015 article on the website For The Church, pastor and professor David Prince mounted a biblical and historic defense of Christian happiness, writing:

> Whatever one thinks of this approach in pitting happiness against Christian sanctification, it must be acknowledged that it is a novel perspective among Christians throughout the ages. Most Christian teachers have taught a vital and indivisible relationship between joy and happiness and between holiness and happiness.[4]

Prince went on to quote Christians from the church fathers to John Piper and Randy Alcorn in defense of the inextricable connection between holiness and happiness.

The important thing we have to remember, however, is that

our priority must not be a particular feeling but a particular fellowship—a close communion with him that is the wellspring of deep, abiding happiness, the kind that cannot come from any earthly circumstances or temporary pleasures.

I will say more about the connection between our emotions and our relationship with God in our coverage of Lie #4, but for now it is enough to reaffirm that God doesn't just want us to be happy, but neither is he disinterested in our happiness. Discerning the biblical truth between these extremes is a key gambit against the devil's wiles. And this also entails discerning the difference between how we typically think of happiness and how the Bible speaks of happiness.

THE DIFFERENCE BETWEEN
HAPPINESS AND JOY

Much has been made of the distinction between "happiness" and "joy," and many find it an arbitrary distinction. David Prince, for instance, wrote:

> Perhaps "happiness" is used in ways that are a bit broader than "joy," but the terms are virtually synonymous. Most theological dictionary definitions of "joy" describe it by using the word "happiness."[5]

In the Scriptures, yes, they are typically synonymous. But this is definitely not the case in modern parlance. This is one of the problems with Victoria Osteen's assertion. Context is everything.

In today's manner of speaking, we think of happiness as the

pleasurable emotion elicited by people, things, and experiences. When I get a raise, I am happier than when I don't. When my kids make good grades, I am happier than when they don't. When my wife gives me a kiss when I get home from work, I am happier than when she doesn't. When sad things happen, I am sad. When happy things happen, I am happy. This is what is called being a normal human being, in which I respond accordingly to positive or negative circumstances in my life. This is generally what people mean today when they speak of happiness.

The Bible leaves much room for this human normality—see Ecclesiastes, for instance, where people are encouraged to enjoy the good gifts of earth God bestows on us all (Eccl. 3:13)—but this is not the kind of happiness the Bible *promises* us through our faith in Jesus. No, in fact, to follow Christ is in essence to take up the work of spiritual crucifixion every day (Luke 9:23), often through some very unhappy places. Nowhere are we encouraged to have a martyr's complex or act happy about sad circumstances. But we are commanded to rejoice in all circumstances (Phil. 4:4; 1 Thess. 5:16). Therefore, joy must be different than (the circumstantial kind of) happiness.

What is joy?

Joy is the music that plays when our hearts are tuned to the frequency of God's glory and our connection to it. Joy is the heart's settled and worshipful contentment in our justification with God. Joy is the conviction that, no matter the sadness of our circumstances or the weakness of our bodies, we are secure in the sovereign God who loves us.

Do you see how joy runs deeper than mere happiness? Happiness is dependent upon our circumstances. Joy is dependent upon our Savior.

This is why, though sad times are promised to believers (John 16:33), we are also promised the gift of joy (John 15:11; Gal. 5:22).

THE KIND OF HAPPINESS JESUS PROMISES

The devil promises joy too. "Eat this fruit," he urges us in a million different ways every day. He holds out the promise of fulfillment, beauty, enlightenment. All the things that run deeper than fleeting pleasures. But his promise is just as fleeting. He wants us to find in the gifts what can only be found in the Giver.

Satan and his minions cannot create anything good. And many times what they tempt us with is not really something forbidden, but something good that might be had *in a way that is forbidden*. God declares sex a good gift to be enjoyed only between a husband and a wife. But years go by, life grows routine, the sex life gets a little stale or even nonexistent. Why would God want us to miss out on a good thing he made? He created those nerve endings, didn't he? And would he want us to be so miserable? A little peek here at someone else, a little taste there of something else . . . what's the harm?

It's not the sex that's bad. It's the perversion of it.

In his classic fictional work on spiritual warfare, *The Screwtape Letters*, C. S. Lewis imagined a senior demon (Screwtape) corresponding with one of his protégés (his nephew Wormwood) as the latter seeks to tempt and afflict his Christian subject. The book is brilliant for its insights into satanic wiles and applications for the Christian's alertness against them. In one of the letters, Uncle Screwtape coaches his pupil on the perversion of pleasure, reminding him that the sin they hold out is tantalizing in part because it corresponds to something their Enemy (God) has actually made for good:

> I know we have won many a soul through pleasure. All the same it is His invention, not ours. He made the pleasures: all our research so far has not enabled us to produce one. All we can do is to encourage the humans to take the pleasures which our Enemy has produced, at times, or in ways, or in degrees, which He has forbidden. Hence we always try to work away from the natural condition of any pleasure to that in which it is least natural, least redolent of its Maker, and least pleasurable. An ever increasing craving for an ever diminishing pleasure is the formula.[6]

Anyone who has given up a succession of inches along the road to degrading themselves knows the feeling. It's there with porn, it's there with food, it's there with literally any other good gift we abuse in the search of fulfillment, beauty, and enlightenment. It takes more and more to achieve the same high. Idolatry is drug abuse.

But when we orient ourselves around the Son, the solar system of our desires and appetites falls into alignment, everything orbiting the center of he who is joy personified.

"Until now you have asked for nothing in my name," he said to his followers. "Ask and you will receive, so that your joy may be complete" (John 16:24).

You and I live daily within an external—and internal—clash of two worldviews. This is the exact tension within which Jesus himself ministered during his earthly tenure. There is the worldview we might call *materialism*, which even Jesus' followers can't seem to keep themselves away from and in which the entire unbelieving world continues to swim. And then there's the worldview of Christianity. So many of the disciples' problems arise from confusing the worldview of Christianity with the worldview of materialism. And so many of our problems arise from also confusing these worldviews. It's one reason why taking verses such as John 16:23–24 out of context can be so appealing, even though we're not doing it intentionally.

The worldview of materialism thinks along these lines:

1. Mankind's greatest need is to have his desires (or feelings) met.
2. Therefore we need things, experiences, and achievements to meet those desires.
3. And then we will be happy.

It begins with our desires (or appetites). It assumes that having "stuff" will satisfy these desires. And when we have these desires met, we will be happy.

Christianity, on the other hand (as I have said), isn't totally disinterested in our desires or feelings—it definitely speaks to those things—but it starts and goes much deeper than any other worldview can. Christianity teaches along these lines:

1. Mankind's greatest need isn't unmet desires but unrealized glory. Our biggest problem isn't unsatisfied feelings but sin. We are disconnected from God and fall short of his glory because of our disobedience and rebellion against him.
2. Therefore, what we need is not a thing, an experience, or an achievement, but salvation, redemption, forgiveness,

righteousness, and rescue—we primarily need the glory of Christ.

3. Once we have Christ (by faith), regardless of our circumstances or feelings (happy or sad), we can have something that runs much deeper than circumstantial feelings. We can have joy. "Fullness of joy," in fact.

So materialism offers circumstantial experiences and temporary things to satisfy superficial desires. Christianity offers the glory of Christ to satisfy the eternal void inside of our souls.

The problem with the materialistic worldview is that it doesn't go deep enough. We're all searching for happiness, but Jesus is offering a deep, bottomless, abounding, everlasting well of forever-joy.

Like the disciples, many times we think we're treasuring Jesus, but we only see the Jesus we want to see, the Jesus we *want* him to be. He knows that when we face the prospect of immense sadness—as did the disciples in the three days of his crucifixion and burial—we may be undone with confusion and pain.

Jesus knows that his followers have to endure a very difficult life in this expansion of his mission since his ascension. They are threatened, accused, exiled, in some cases tortured, and in many cases executed for their faith.

But he makes them a promise. He makes them a promise that is far greater than earthly rewards and earthly successes.

Truly I tell you, you will weep and mourn, but the world will rejoice. You will become sorrowful, but your sorrow will turn to joy. When a woman is in labor, she has pain because her time has come. But when she has given birth to a child, she no

THE GOSPEL ACCORDING TO SATAN

longer remembers the suffering because of the joy that a person has been born into the world. So you also have sorrow now. But I will see you again. Your hearts will rejoice, and no one will take away your joy from you. (John 16:20–22)

The pain is a promise. And, reader, *your* pain is a promise.

One day your tears not only will be wiped away but will turn to rapturous joy. He will trade your ashes for beauty. Every single hurt you endure will be stored up and returned to you a million-fold in heavenly bliss.

With that in mind, let us turn to the little theology of prayer Jesus offered there in John 16:

In that day you will not ask me anything. Truly I tell you, anything you ask the Father in my name, he will give you. Until now you have asked for nothing in my name. Ask and you will receive, so that your joy may be complete. (vv. 23–24)

Whenever we pray—or whenever we expect something from God—we face the clash of worldviews. Will we walk by sight—materialism? Or will we walk by faith—true Christianity? The key phrase in this passage is the repeated "in my name." It is directly connected to God's ultimate priority for us, which is holiness reflective of his ultimate priority for himself, which is glory.

Sometimes people treat this prayer like magic words. "The reason you still suffer is because you don't have enough faith," they say. Or, "The reason you haven't gotten what you want is because you're not praying hard enough." But this is satanic. We cannot add "in Jesus' name" and get what we want. God is not some kind of cosmic vending machine for our hopes and dreams. The whole point of John 16:23–24 is that our hopes and dreams are not the point. The point is the glory of Jesus Christ!

When you ask anything "in the name of Jesus," what that really means is that you want the name of Jesus to be magnified more than anything. And if that means the Father must say no to your requests—for healing, for comfort, for "stuff," for *happiness*—it means the no is better than the yes, if only the name of Christ is exalted.

Whatever you want, Lord, we want! Whatever most brings you glory, Jesus, that's what we want.

The promise is that if you will align your purposes and ambitions and prayer requests with God's purposes, you still may fail but he never will. And in the end, your sorrow will turn into joy.

I told you in a footnote that the story of Gretchen was a composite of numerous similar conversations I've had with same-sex attracted friends. Some of those Gretchens found my answers wanting. Most of them admitted to wanting to believe the Bible. Some of them disagreed with me on what the Bible says about homosexuality. Some agreed with me that the Bible forbids any acting on homosexual desires, but they decided they didn't care. They wanted to appreciate God's Word, not obey it!

Yet still others have forged the way, with God's help, toward difficult belief. They have embraced the hardship of dying to themselves and taking up their crosses daily.

A couple of Gretchens I know are living quite fulfilling lives, subjecting their desires to God's Word and following his design for men and women. I sometimes wonder why heterosexual Christians think that doing this should be so easy. It may be because they are not quite doing it themselves.

To find your life, you must lose it. Jesus said so (Matt. 10:39).

He wants you to have the eternal joy of himself, not simply the fleeting happiness of your flesh.

So many of us have our hearts set on temporary happiness. And that's fine as far as that goes. You'd be weird if you only wanted to be sad all the time. You'd be abnormal if you enjoyed getting hurt! So pray for healing, pray for comfort, pray for things you need. But remember that true joy—which you can have despite your hurt, despite your trials, despite your poverty, despite your lack—can be had in any circumstance because you have Christ, who will never leave you nor forsake you. He will never let you go.

This is the only safe "bet," and it is infinitely more pleasurable than whatever the devil is offering. God doesn't "just" want you to be happy; he wants you to be holy as he is holy and to find true, lasting joy in him.

YOU ONLY LIVE ONCE

You will not die.

—THE SERPENT

I WAS A PRETTY SMART HIGH SCHOOL KID AND fairly well-behaved, too, but occasionally I engaged in some of the stupidest things ever done by stupid people. Such things usually involved buddies, not one of whom was as stupid as the collective group of us. As Tommy Lee Jones says in the movie *Men in Black*, "A *person* is smart. *People* are dumb." There was no one among us to say, "Hey, this is really stupid."

How stupid were we?

On a handful of nights over our senior year, we would pile into Mike's car and drive around the suburban neighborhoods of northwest Houston with Nicky in the trunk. I would sit in the passenger seat while Mike drove, a baseball bat in my lap. We would amble through a vast array of well-manicured lawns and brick mailboxes until some poor soul ended up behind us, at which point we would wait until we came to a stop sign.

At the stop sign, with the car behind us simply waiting its turn, I would reach into the glove compartment and pop the trunk. Nicky would "escape."

If you can picture the strange sight of someone emerging from the trunk of a vehicle in front of you at a stop sign, imagine also the stranger sight of the passenger of that vehicle—this would be me—jumping out of the car, bat in hand, to "recapture" the escapee. After a few half-convincing blows to the stomach and back with the bat, I would rustle Nicky back into the trunk, slam it shut, and jump back into the passenger seat, and then we would race off.

I told you it was stupid.

We did this maybe five or six times, and at no point did it occur to any of us that it was stupid—only that it was freaking hilarious.

To the people behind us? Not so much.

We had people lay on their horns, people scream, people shout. One guy even began chasing us through the neighborhood. (Nicky was lucky to have that guy so concerned about him.) We eventually stopped but only because the person who chased us happened to be an off-duty police officer. He didn't catch us, but he did catch Mike's license plate number. Fortunately, this officer knew it was a stupid prank and that he wasn't witnessing an almost-botched kidnapping. So he merely gave Mike a call and told him officially, on behalf of the Harris County Sheriff's Department, that we were stupid and should knock it off before someone got hurt.

This was the early 1990s, before everyone had mobile phones

to call the police or, I guess, upload our shenanigans to YouTube. But this was Texas. Meaning nobody had phones, but plenty of people had guns. I suppose it was only God's kind favor that I hadn't ended up bringing a Louisville Slugger to a gunfight.

If you're a young person reading this, thinking it sounds very funny—well, you're right. It is pretty funny. But it was also dangerous and, as I said, supremely *stupid*. But, hey, you're only young once. Do you really want to go through your whole life without doing a few stupid things once in a while?

If not, you should.

This is kind of the point of the entire biblical book of Proverbs. Most of Proverbs is written from the perspective of a dad, presumably with his arm around his son's shoulder, showing his son how not to be stupid. "Son, watch out for the trapdoor of lust. And also for your idiot buddies." That's the basic gist of Proverbs, and it's a common theme through all of the "wisdom literature" of the Bible, so called because it is mostly written in song and verse and reflects a more philosophical style than the prophetic or narrative books. God is very determined that we navigate our lives *wisely*. As opposed to stupidly.

> Listen, my son, to your father's instruction,
> and don't reject your mother's teaching,
> for they will be a garland of favor on your head
> and pendants around your neck. (Prov. 1:8–9)

As far as bodily accoutrements go, a garland and a pendant are perhaps not as cutting edge as a YOLO tattoo, but what they make up for in timelessness they lack in stupidity.

You don't hear the YOLO ("you only live once") cheer too

much anymore. Like every other bit of hashtag wisdom, its hallowed place in pop culture lasted about as long as a fart. In just a few brief moments YOLO went from hip-hop's version of *carpe diem* to just one more social media in-joke, the subject of countless ironic status updates and sarcastic memes.

In the 1989 Peter Weir film *Dead Poets Society*, Robin Williams plays an eccentric and inspiring teacher of English lit who famously tells his students at the traditional boarding school, "Seize the day, boys. Make your lives extraordinary." This was perhaps the first popularization of YOLO in our modern era. Williams's Professor Keating was inspired by the poetry of Walt Whitman and Robert Herrick, as well as the beauty of nature itself. Three decades on, however, adherents to the assertion that "you only live once" seem more inspired by sex, money, and materialism.

The rappers didn't invent this, though. The devil did.

STUPID IS AS STUPID DOESN'T

It was not a conscious apprehension of our youthfulness that drove Mike, Nicky, and me to carry out that silly playacting in front of hapless motorists in Houston, but it was definitely, if maybe only subconsciously, an embrace of our youthfulness: an implicit acknowledgment that throughout the history of time, young men with lots of energy have done crazy things, and "Hey! *We* were young men with lots of energy." We weren't thinking about the possible ramifications; we were just enjoying being teenage boys doing what teenage boys do. What we weren't doing was thinking at all. We were simply seizing the day.

That central conceit of *Dead Poets Society*—*carpe diem* ("seize the day")—comes from the Herrick poem "To the Virgins, to Make Much of Time," which reads in part:

> Gather ye rose-buds while ye may,
> Old Time is still a-flying;
> And this same flower that smiles today
> Tomorrow will be dying.

In other words, life is short, and it will soon be over. Pick that flower while it's blooming. It will be too late when it's dead. Make the most of your time, and enjoy it while you have it.

You could contrast this verse with any selection of lyrics from the Drake song "The Motto," but there is no complete thought from which I could, in good conscience, reprint here. My kids may be reading this. If you have a high tolerance for explicit language and graphic sexuality, you could Google the song. (Please don't say I didn't warn you.) Or perhaps you've already heard it. We all do dumb things now and again, so don't be too embarrassed. In any event, our modern poet Drake waxes poetic around the YOLO theme (the song's titular "motto") in talking about clubbing, having sex with anonymous women, making millions of dollars, and having more sex with anonymous women.

He's a very original guy, this Drake.

No, not really. We can trace all of this—seizing the day, gathering the rosebuds, having as much indiscriminate sex as possible—right to sentiments documented in the Bible. Isaiah 22:13 comes to mind: "Let us eat and drink, for tomorrow we die!"

I mean, what's the point of life if not to enjoy yourself while you can? This seems to be the working thesis behind the thoughts examined in Ecclesiastes 8:14–15:

There is a futility that is done on the earth: there are righteous people who get what the actions of the wicked deserve,
and there are wicked people who get what the actions of the
righteous deserve. I say that this too is futile. So I commended
enjoyment because there is nothing better for a person under
the sun than to eat, drink, and enjoy himself, for this will
accompany him in his labor during the days of his life that
God gives him under the sun.

The consideration of futility is important there. Doing good
hardly seems to get rewarded. Doing bad hardly seems to matter.
So why not just do what you want with the time you've got? Why
not simply do what you feel?

One of the great things about all the wisdom books in the
Bible is that they accurately depict the way our minds work. We
really do think this way. We may not live like that as a normal
course of life, but from time to time we justify little rebellions
here and there, excuse this or that disobedience. Who will notice?
What difference does it make?

And the other great thing about all the wisdom books is that
they show us how stupid it is to think this way, how thinking this
way isn't really thinking at all. The logic of "eat and drink, for
tomorrow you die" doesn't take in all the facts. It is operating at
the level of appetite only and not on the level of wisdom.

Wisdom weighs all the facts, not just the convenient ones.

In Genesis 3, the woman says to the serpent that if she eats
the forbidden fruit, the Lord says she will die.

"No, you won't," the serpent replies.

The only thing more stupid than not thinking beyond death
is not thinking about death at all.

"This is next-level stuff," he promises her.

And the woman, knowing what God has said, conveniently ignores the facts he's given her, seeing only the allure of the prospect before her. "Let me eat and be merry," she appears to think, "for even if I die, it won't be till tomorrow."

Sin is fundamentally stupid. Oh, it has that logic of immediacy to it, the appealing apparent sensibility of pleasure—of fulfillment, beauty, and enlightenment—but it always bids us make the most of time by wasting it. The temptations you and I face every day carry the same convoluted logic:

- "You deserve this."
- "They deserve you doing this to them."
- "It's just a little taste, a little peek, a little pleasure."
- "Nobody will get hurt."
- "This will give you relief."
- "This will make you happy."
- "Look, you only live once."

And then we choose bit by bit a piece of death, believing it will give us life. "You won't die," the sin promises. But then you do. We all do.

The convoluted logic of sin is that it makes the indulgence seem urgent, pressing, as not indulging would be to miss out, to store up regret for later, all the while trying to convince us that later will never come. "You only live once" is profoundly stupid in that the risks it gives rise to imply you will live forever.

This is also why I've never understood the concept of the bucket list. People fill their list with things like bungee jumping, sky diving, free-climbing Yosemite, and I think to myself, *You*

*know, for someone trying to get things done before you die, it sure
sounds like you've got a death wish.*

It is wisdom to make the most of the time that is given to
us, yes. But it is wisdom to know that the time given to us is a
lot longer than we think it is. The stupid think that you only live
once. The wise know that we only get one life, and what we do
with it matters because of what comes after.

Seize the day, yes, but seize it in light of what comes when you
run out of days to seize.

ONLY GOD CAN JUDGE YOU, AND HE WILL

YOLO has a couple of stupid buddies. One of them is "no regrets."
I especially find it emotionally delicious when this is expressed in a
misspelled tattoo, "No Regerts" being a personal favorite. The idea
behind "no regrets" is similar to "you only live once," predicated
as they both are in self-centered, self-willed hedonistic indulgence.

I understand that many people who say "no regrets" are thinking of how to make the best use of their days in terms of spending
quality time with family and doing good in the world, but far too
often, it becomes a stand-in for "eat, drink, and be merry." In any
event, it is impossible for those of soft conscience to truly live a
life free of regrets. No wise person could ever live with no regrets.
Having regrets is for those who learn from their mistakes and
grieve their sins. "No regrets" is for people with no conscience.
Only sociopaths have no regrets.

The other stupid buddy is "only God can judge me." I've seen
this one on car window decals, in Facebook graphics and Instagram
captions, and even on airbrushed T-shirts. (I don't know about

God, but I definitely judge that last one.) What always strikes me as funny is that those who say "only God can judge me" are usually the kind of people living as if he won't.

You put these three idiots—"You only live once," "No regrets," and "Only God can judge me"—in a car together on a Friday night, and they're going to cook up some seriously stupid ideas.

"It is appointed for people to die once," Hebrews 9:27 says, "and after this, judgment." So sure, live up this one life you've got. Just remember that the whole thing is spent with time that is borrowed. Back in Ecclesiastes, the guy with the YOLO tattoo gets a strong dose of reality:

> Rejoice, young person, while you are young,
>   and let your heart be glad in the days of your youth.
> And walk in the ways of your heart
>   and in the desire of your eyes;
> but know that for all of these things God will bring you
>   to judgment. (11:9)

What Satan would love for you to do is spend this life as if that's all there is. First, he won't want you to think about death at all, not even if it brings you a sense of dread. The devil likes to traffic in fear, but it's not his immediate go-to, because he knows that fearful people often cry out for help, which means fearful people are very close to having their ears open to divine rescue. Instead, he wants you to think of death as some far-off thing, not a big deal, certainly nothing that could happen tomorrow or in the next five minutes. He wants you drunk on a sense of immortality. This comes somewhat naturally to teenagers, boys especially, but it persists in a kind of perpetual teenagerdom in Western culture where youth is idolized and immortality is sold in little packets by pyramid-scheming soccer moms and discounted by "lifestyle gyms" every New Year's.

"You only live once, and it might as well be forever." That's the first lie the devil tries.

If that doesn't work—if you insist on acknowledging your own mortality and finitude—he will say, "Okay, okay, yes, you're going to die. And yes, it may in fact be tomorrow. So get as much pleasure as you can! Gather up those rosebuds, even the ones in somebody else's yard, even the ones you're explicitly told not to pick. You've only got one life, and it's way too short to play by the rules." If you won't deny you'll live forever, he will want you focused as much on the here and now as possible, as if death is a great nothingness that threatens to ruin the party.

What the devil absolutely *doesn't* want is for you to consider what comes after death. "You only live once," he insists, not simply as a seize-the-day motivational proverb but as a theological dogmatism. He wants you to stop before you get to the last line of Ecclesiastes 11:9 when "for all of these things God will bring you to judgment."

You may think I'm overselling this. But "you only live once" isn't only the motto of adolescent knuckleheads and adult thrill seekers. It's the motto of every man whose investment in the future is limited to his retirement plan and the material benefits he leaves his family. It's the motto of every mom whose chief concern for her children is that they end up healthy, in a good school, or with a respectable spouse. It's the motto of every person who goes through life never thinking of what comes after their last breath.

"You only live once" is the subconscious affirmation of every person, like you or me, who spends their day overwhelmingly anxious about the troubles of the day, as if *this is it*.

Life is precious, and each human soul is sacred. Which is why "you only live once" is too cheap a philosophy for us to buy into.

Jesus himself said, "Don't fear those who kill the body but are not able to kill the soul; rather, fear him who is able to destroy both soul and body in hell" (Matt. 10:28).

What he means is, dying isn't the worst thing that can happen to you. Dying *after you die* is the worst thing that can happen to you. The second death is far worse—infinitely worse—than the first. Satan will do whatever is in his power to keep you from thinking about that.

What we do in this life matters far beyond a series of accumulations or our senses of pleasure. It's not that doing enough good deeds will help you avoid hell. That's another false gospel the devil likes to preach. And there are plenty of people who do good deeds only to prop up the idol of themselves. This is as much a storing up of wrath for eternity as a life of outward sin.

We are all going to die. Nobody gets out of this world alive. You may die with six-pack abs and a marathoner's endurance, but you will be worm food. And then you will kneel before a holy God who rises to judge what's become of your life. Did you waste it focusing only on yourself, giving no thought to this moment?

He will look at your good and bad, but there will be no scales. If you live like "only God can judge me," don't be surprised when he does. If you spend your life fixated on your life and not trusting in the one who *is* Life (John 14:6), you will surely die.

The reality is that the eternal life we receive through faith in Jesus is exactly that—eternal. This means that we can live lives today with the quality of eternality, if only because the God of the universe has incarnated himself in this world and, after his ascension to heaven, sent his Spirit to fill the "eternity in [our] hearts" (Eccl. 3:11).

The devil doesn't even care whether you're religious, so long as you don't believe that; therefore, we must reject his false gospel of this-life-onlyism. We must not think only of seizing the day but, in the day to day, taking hold of eternity.

SEIZE ETERNITY TO SPITE THE DEVIL

A couple of years ago I read Matthew McCullough's book *Remember Death*, but I almost stopped in the introduction when I read these lines:

> In our time and place, death isn't something we think about
> very often, if at all. . . . I'm writing to convince those living like
> immortals that they're not actually immortal. . . . I'm writing
> to those for whom death feels remote and unreal—something
> that happens to other people.[1]

Why did I almost stop reading? Because this does not describe me. I think about death every day. In the ministry of my most recent pastorate, I helped bury saint after saint, friend after friend. I preached at countless funerals. I held the hands of one friend after another as they took their last breaths. Death was thrust upon me.

And I think about my death every day. I don't know if it's because of the heaviness of my ministry experience, the heaviness of my own melancholy personality, or simply the heaviness of entering my middle-age years, but not a day goes by that I don't think about when I'll go, how I'll go, and where I'll go.

McCullough was explicitly saying he had not written his book for someone like me. But I read on. Why? Because I don't need to simply remember death but to remember my life. I kept reading because I am always keen on reliable guides to the horizon of eternity. I am glad I kept reading, because I encountered valuable truths like this:

> Glory [is not] transient but eternal. Not vaporous but weighty. Not fragmented and fleeting, but joy fulfilled and forever. Because whatever glory may be like, it is defined by the presence of God himself, apart from whom there is no good thing.[2]

Ah, but we're afraid there are no good things to come! Or at least no good things comparable to the good things to be had in this world. But the exact opposite is true. The good pleasures of this world are only signposts to the greater bliss of heaven. They cannot really compare to them, and therefore they must never replace them. I don't care how tasty Jacob's red stew was; it still wasn't worth the birthright! As John Piper said, "Life is too short, too precious, too painful to waste on worldly bubbles that burst. Heaven is too great, hell is too horrible, eternity is too long that we should putter around on the porch of eternity."[3]

All that endless accumulation? All that self-determinism? All that YOLO, "No regrets," "Only God can judge me" self-revering gobbledygook? It's just a puttering around on the porch. To borrow from C. S. Lewis, it's a messing around with mud puddles, ignorant of the beach just around the corner.

The devil wants you on the porch. His "gospel" will point out all the fine architectural features, all the room to play. "Just pay no attention to what's beyond the door behind you."

We must spite him, you and I. We must remember the judgment that's coming, the judgment that matters. We must remember death, yes, but also what comes after.

I wish I could get into a time machine and go back to one night in 1993, stop myself before I got into Mike's car, and give myself a copy of McCullough's *Remember Death*. Or just point myself to Ecclesiastes. "You're not going to live forever, pal. Make good choices. Don't be stupid."

I probably wouldn't have listened. One reason stupid people are stupid is because they mostly listen to stupid messages.

So, by all means, seize the day if you're just interested in having a little fun. Seize eternity if you're interested in living forever. There's a motto for that too.

LIVE ONCE, DIE TWICE; LIVE TWICE, DIE ONCE

A religious expert once came to Jesus to ask about the kingdom of God. The religious experts had a huge stake in the answers to the "kingdom of God" questions. They had carved out a niche with rules and regulations related to how you could enter and remain in the kingdom. A lot had to do with what you did.

Jesus said to the man, "Unless someone is born again, he cannot see the kingdom of God" (John 3:3). It was a weird thing to say, and even the religious expert could not make heads or tails of it. He wanted to know how a grown man could go back into his mother's womb and be reborn.

You can be very religious and still fall for the devil's lie that this life is all that matters.

Jesus is of course referring to the second birth, the new birth in him—or put another way, the "living twice"—that happens when we repent of our sin and believe in the good news of his sinless life, sacrificial death, and glorious resurrection. This new birth requires a death of our old selves and all its old ways of seeking fulfillment, beauty, and enlightenment anywhere but in Jesus. This new birth requires that we "die to ourselves" and thereby find new life in him (Rom. 6:8; Gal. 2:20; 2 Tim. 2:11).

Live once, die twice. Live twice, die once. No, it's not as catchy as YOLO. I'm not even sure how you'd pronounce it. (Lod-tell-tee-doo?) But as far as clichés go, "live once, die twice; live twice, die once" is a whole lot more biblical than the alternative.

To reject Jesus is to reject real life, as he himself is life. To choose to "do life" without him is to choose a death worse than death: to choose the second death, the spiritual death that comes after physical death. And the spiritual death is far worse. But to choose Christ this side of death is to have him forever. You may die physically, but those who live in Christ live forever. They have "eternal life" (John 3:16).

Ergo: Live once, die twice. Live twice, die once.

Like we do, Jesus' closest followers often struggled with these concepts. Like the religious experts, they had grown accustomed to thinking of the kingdom as pertaining mostly to the here and now. This gave rise to both zealous revolutionaries and compromising sellouts. All along the journey of Christ's ministry, his friends at various moments expected Jesus would begin violently overthrowing the oppressors and "setting up shop" in Jerusalem.

This even appears to be part of the devil's temptations against him in the wilderness (Matt. 4:6–9).

So all along the way, Jesus is constantly rebuking the this-world focus of his disciples. Sometimes he does it gently, and sometimes he does it harshly. But he always does it lovingly, because, unlike Satan, he actually loves these people. He wants what is best for them. In Mark 8:36, he said to them, "For what does it benefit someone to gain the whole world and yet lose his life?"

The enemy wants us to answer "everything."

But Jesus wants what is best for you. He knows living like you only live once is to ensure you will die after you die.

You must be born again. Because if you live once, you will die twice. But if you live twice, you will die once. And after that, everlasting glory.

The fruit of the now looks pretty pathetic in the light of eternal life.

Dying twice is the only way to live forever. The devil wants us to believe we won't die. Barring that, he wants us to believe only this life counts, that *this* is all there is. But he's a liar. He wants us to waste this life, because he wants us to waste what comes after. As C. S. Lewis wrote in his mythic retelling *Till We Have Faces*, "Die before you die. There is no chance after."[4]

After we die it will be too late to change our minds. It will be too late to get our act together. This is why Solomon told those who are young to remember their Creator now, in the days of their youth (Eccl. 12:1). There is no moment to delay. Gather the rosebuds of eternity while ye may! If you have not done so already, seize eternity this very second.

YOU NEED TO LIVE
YOUR TRUTH

*The mind is its own place, and in it self
Can make a Heav'n of Hell, a Hell of Heav'n.*
—JOHN MILTON, *PARADISE LOST*

THE TRUTH IS CENTERING. THE TRUTH IS STABILIZ-
ing. The truth is clarifying. That is, if we are willing to upend our
devotion to our preferred version of the truth. If we are not, the
truth is disorienting, disturbing, and confounding.

If you're like me, you've had plenty of lies told about you.
You've suffered from hearing about various versions of you pre-
sented by others. In such cases, you find that telling the truth
doesn't seem to help.

I once had a fellow in my church stand up in a business

meeting and announce to everyone that I had told him a particular thing that I had, in fact, never said. I don't know where he got his version of the truth from. Wanting to assume the best, I chalked it up to mishearing or misunderstanding. But not only did I not say the thing he told everyone I said, I *wouldn't* have said the thing he told everyone I said. It was so far from the truth that it didn't even reflect anything I *might* have said.

I corrected him. I told the truth.

"Well, that's what I heard," he said, shocked that I would apparently lie in front of my church.

It became a matter of "he said / he said." The truth, as far as the congregation was concerned, depended upon which one of us they found more credible, more trustworthy. Lines were drawn.

It was not a huge thing. It had to do with the formation of a certain committee. But he was citing my alleged statement as evidence against my care for the church. And it became bigger than the statement at hand. We both agreed to let the matter drop—publicly, at least—but the damage had been done.

People believe what they want to believe. And this is why truth is so hard to come by these days.

The current president of the United States lies just about every day on his Twitter feed. Many Americans have just come to accept this as part of the social contract we enter into with our politicians. Of course, if the politician in question is not one you voted for or currently support, it's an egregious ethical breach and sin against the American people. But if he or she is on your side, you just consider it the trade-off we make for achieving certain policy goals (or preventing certain policy goals from the other side).

Donald Trump didn't invent dishonesty in politics, of course. It's even older than Bill Clinton's hemming and hawing about what the meaning of "is" is. But our modern politicos and pundits have turned dishonesty into an art form, even a new language, that suits the increasingly self-reverential spirit of the age.

It's a strange thing, too, because now more than ever we have access to facts, to concrete records of statements and events. Nearly everything we do and say is somehow broadcast on the Internet or otherwise imprinted for posterity. Those old emails? They will find you out. Those offhand remarks in a staff meeting or off-mic at a press conference? They will show up again. Those who aren't publishing their every thought are being recorded by everybody else who wants your thoughts published.

We dissect context, nuance, circumstance, intonation, semantics—all in seeking to indict or exonerate ourselves and others. A celebrity is caught saying something awful about minorities or victims, and he claims he was taken out of context. Caught with the facts, he may claim, "That wasn't the real me."

We have made extraordinary advances in playing fast and loose with the truth.

And the devil is loving it.

THE TRUTH IS OUT THERE

We are a couple of decades past the vastly popular initial run of the TV show *The X-Files*, but its themes continue to resonate. In the show, two FBI agents, Fox Mulder and Dana Scully, investigate paranormal claims that somehow all trace back to an interconnected web of conspiracies involving extraterrestrials and clandestine branches of the United States government. Mulder and Scully represented two facets of our psyche: he the "true believer" and she the skeptic.

"I want to believe" read a poster featuring a UFO on Mulder's office wall. "Show me the facts," Scully said in so many words on each investigation.

The deeper they went, the more complex the conspiracy seemed to get—and the more convoluted for viewers like me. But still they soldiered on, wide-eyed interest and narrow-minded scrutiny working side by side to finally get to the bottom of the truth. By the end of the program and throughout a couple of theatrical movies and TV miniseries revivals, Mulder and Scully had switched places. The true believer had become hardened, grizzled, much more of a skeptic. He was tired of the search. The skeptic, on the other hand, had had her mind more and more opened by things she'd seen. She became more open, more "religious."

This dynamic plays out today, I'm convinced, in the current fascination with the true crime genre. In streaming documentaries, investigative news shows, and journalistic podcasts, we are exploring "cold cases" and perplexing disappearances with an increasing amount of obsessiveness.

There is something about the mystery that drives us. Somebody has to know something. The facts have to add up to something.

I confess that almost every day I check key word searches on three unsolved crimes that have particularly affected me. It has become routine to search for any news or developments in two murder cases and one disappearance. You may not be so compelled, but you've probably watched *Making a Murderer* or *The Staircase* on Netflix. Or you've clicked on yet another link about the murder of JonBenet Ramsey or the mysteries of the Zodiac Killer or D. B. Cooper.

There's something about the search that is itself satisfying.

Why? Because we know the truth is out there and we believe, despite the daily deception we accept as part of living in the modern world, that finding it is worth it. Justice is at stake.

The religious world Jesus entered was one that had become fractious with fact claims. The Roman Empire of course operated on a kind of reasonable philosophy but still maintained a tie to the sentimental religion of polytheism and emperor worship. Against the backdrop of this Roman dominion, the Jews found themselves splintered into various groups that were each equally devoted to their truth.

The Essenes had retreated into the desert to dedicate themselves to a gnostic, mystical form of Judaism. The Zealots were the righteous antagonists of their day, stirring up the odd rebellion here and there, thinking violence was the best way to coerce righteousness into the land. The Sadducees, like so many religious pundits today with political stars in their eyes, sold out, compromising the old truth for the new truth of access to power and comfort. The Pharisees seemed to be the lone holdouts, the "true believers" unwilling to compromise and totally committed to the old ways no matter what.

Of all the factions, the Pharisees were somehow the closest to the truth. At least, they were the ones with their noses closest to the facts. But there's something true today that was just as true two thousand years ago: no amount of facts will convince anyone who is committed to disbelief.

You can see the way this refusal to believe plays out in the latter part of John 8. This is where we find that now-legendary phrase "You will know the truth, and the truth will set you free" (v. 32). Those are the words of Jesus, and while they've been co-opted in modern usage to apply to all kinds of searches for truth,

Jesus was referring to belief in himself as Lord of the world and Savior of sinners.

The passage begins by identifying Jesus' words as directed to those who believe in him (v. 31), but the ones who do not believe interject, "We're already free."

What ensues is a wrestling over two versions of the truth. For every word of Jesus, these folks have a counterpoint. They are citing the facts as they see them. "We are not slaves. We are descendants of Abraham. We have one Father."

Right in front of them, however, is the ultimate Fact, the Son of God incarnate. He is the living embodiment of Truth. And he dismantles their interpretation point by point, ultimately crediting their disbelief to satanic influence:

> Jesus said to them, "If God were your Father, you would love me, because I came from God and I am here. For I didn't come on my own, but he sent me. Why don't you understand what I say? Because you cannot listen to my word. You are of your father the devil, and you want to carry out your father's desires. He was a murderer from the beginning and does not stand in the truth, because there is no truth in him. When he tells a lie, he speaks from his own nature, because he is a liar and the father of lies. Yet because I tell the truth, you do not believe me. Who among you can convict me of sin? If I am telling the truth, why don't you believe me? The one who is from God listens to God's words. This is why you don't listen, because you are not from God." (John 8:42–47)

These are very harsh words, to be sure, and Jesus' opponents respond with one of the oldest tactics from the schoolyards of yore, basically saying, "I know you are, but what am I?" Seriously. After Jesus attributes their disbelief to demonic influence, they respond in verse 48 by basically saying, "Aren't *you* the one with a demon?"

Jesus doubles down, denying their version of the truth and reiterating his. "Truly I tell you . . ." (v. 51).

As you can expect, this still does not convince. They double down as well. "Now we know you have a demon" (v. 52).

The stakes were already high. Now they are even higher. This is not simply a religious squabble between an upstart rabbi and the old-guard politicians. This isn't two tribes trolling each other on Twitter. This is good and evil squaring off; this is eternal life and death.

Jesus is interpreting the facts for them. The facts they claim to know. He is shining the light of himself on them, showing that he is the solution to the mystery! Further, he is the fulfillment of the longing they feel. He is the apex of the beautiful glory they seek. He is the arrival of the enlightenment they claim to already have. And with the truth standing right in front of them, deflecting their debate points like Neo with those bullets in *The Matrix*, they refuse to believe. So he drops a bomb on them:

"Truly I tell you, before Abraham was, I am" (v. 58).

He has short-circuited them. They are out of words. He has messed with not only their version of the facts but their sense of knowing itself. Jesus has just disrupted the space-time continuum. Having lost the battle for the truth, they pick up rocks to kill him (v. 59). And somehow, mysteriously, Jesus disappears from their midst.

The truth is out there.

THE FATHER OF LIES IS A
MASTER OF DEFLECTION

In the previous chapter, I argued that one of the devil's go-to gambits is keeping us stupid. What's especially insidious about this ploy, however, is that the kind of stupid the devil wants for us doesn't really have anything to do with intellect. "The fool says in his heart, 'There's no God'" (Ps. 14:1; 53:1). Clearly, the biblical kind of foolishness is not the same as unintelligence, as you and I likely know plenty of intelligent atheists and unbelievers of all kinds.

No, the atheist isn't always a fool in his mind but is instead a fool *in his heart*. And it's not simply those who intellectually discount the existence of God who carry this kind of atheistic foolishness around in their hearts. When we engage in the biblical kind of foolishness—choosing sin over obedience—we engage in a practical kind of atheism. We give our hearts to someone or something else. We say with our hearts that there is no God worthy of our allegiance, no God worthy of the glory we are denying him, no God who will hold us accountable. Behavior problems are belief problems.

So the justifications we offer for ourselves and our sins are usually pretty sophisticated or, at the least, pretty wordy. We have convinced ourselves that we are right, despite the word from God to the contrary. Others have misread it. We have the real facts. It doesn't apply to us or to this circumstance specifically. We are the exception for whatever reason. We have to live "our truth."

Paul told Timothy that people who believe this way do not have real "knowledge of the truth" (2 Tim. 2:25) and need to "come to their senses" (v. 26). That latter phrasing is a tip-off to how drunk we can be even on our own intellect and still be ignorant of our ignorance. Paul has no problem attributing this nonsense way of living to "the trap of the devil" (v. 26).

The trap is subtle. What Satan continues to do today is what he originally did in the garden: substituting a version of rival facts in place of the real thing. Every sinful decision you and I make begins with the satanic question, "Did God really say . . . ?"

Satan has come with his own spin on the facts. "You won't die. You can become like God. You will know new things and see like him."

These lies appealed to Adam and Eve, we reckon, because they deflected from reality. Satan is not just a master of deception but also a master of deflection. He does not outright say, "Disobey!" No, he distracts. He demurs. He redirects. "What about this?" he says. "What about that? Have you looked at it this way? What if *this* and what about *that*?" He makes the trap look like an endless field of possibilities, a playground of sorts that he suggests God wants to deny you.

Make no mistake. What the devil is after is your allegiance to him by way of your allegiance to yourself, but he rarely starts with that. He starts by reframing your relationship with God. Dietrich Bonhoeffer called mankind's original sin "going behind the given Word of God and procuring his own knowledge of God."[1]

In Matthew 16:23, Jesus called Peter "Satan" not because Peter outright renounced his loyalty to his Master but because he positioned his disbelief (in Christ's crucifixion and resurrection) as *concern* for him. Think of the harsh words Jesus had for and about his family after they'd treated him like a crazy or reckless person. Think of the harsh words he had for his disciples whenever they suggested self-protection or self-fulfillment was the order of the day. "You are a hindrance to me because you're not thinking about

God's concerns but human concerns," Jesus went on to say to Peter. In other words, "You want me to believe this is about your relationship with me, but it's really about your concerns about yourself."

Peter was deflecting. But the truth is centering.

One way the devil deflects us from the truth is by appealing to our senses of virtue, righteousness, or justice. Truth feels cold sometimes, hard. We long for the truth, but sometimes the truth convicts us or just proves too others-oriented.

It is interesting that in 2 Corinthians 2:10–11, Paul referred to unforgiveness as a scheme of Satan. The devil knows that forgiving each other serves the magnification of God, which is the thing Satan hates the most, so he appeals to our sense of justice. "You will just let this guy off scot-free? He doesn't deserve forgiveness. After what he's done? He'll just keep on doing it then, since you're giving him permission. Go ahead, be a doormat. See how far that gets you."

It makes sense. Forgiving people do get taken advantage of. But unforgiving people, Paul said in verse 11, get taken advantage of by Satan!

So there we stand, wronged as all get-out. We've been unjustly treated. We hurt. We want things to be made right. We want justice. And the devil comes along to fester our wounds for us, to offer us sips of his bitter brew. He urges coldness, harshness, vengeance. "What's right is right."

He is trying to reframe the law of God for his own ends, to make himself god vicariously through you.

But the Lord says, "Vengeance is mine; I will repay." The Lord says, "You all have sinned, thus you must all forgive. If the debt has been settled by Christ on the cross, what do you mean by extracting further payment? Is the cross of Christ that cheap to you?"[2]

It is that cheap to Satan. He wants your eyes off the cross, because where your sin and mine has been conquered, so has he.

YOUR TRUTH IS RELATIVE

My friend Gretchen had fallen prey to this lie from Satan: "You are worth this decision. You were made to live this way. You are only affirming how God has designed you." She had decided to live "her truth," in the parlance of our time.

I don't know which celebrity philosopher first thrust this cliché upon us. I know it has been well-worn by Oprah Winfrey. You can search "this is my truth" or "I will live my truth" on social media and find literally thousands of examples, and these are just two variations among hundreds available.

The truth is, there is no "your truth" and "my truth." There is only *the* truth. What we are saying when we say "I only need to live my truth" is that we don't care about the facts as God sees them; we only care about the facts as *we* see them. There is a biblical book that's basically all about this concept—"Everyone doing what was right in their own eyes." It's called Judges, and it's full of bloodshed and perversion. Moral and relational chaos is the natural result of everybody living "their truth."

Now, Gretchen does not agree with that. Her truth speaks differently. Her truth says that everything will be better with her now because she has finally decided to stop living everybody else's truth and live her own. But, as we said in a previous chapter, this way of living also assumes that you only live once. Suppose everything does go well for her in the days and years ahead. Suppose she is happier. Suppose she finds people who share "her truth," people for whom what God says doesn't much affect their way of living, because his words seem so much more stifling than the freedom of their truth. Then suppose they get to the end of a very long, happy life and must face the author of truth who wants to know why they'd trade eternity for, comparatively speaking, a blip on its radar?

The truth, ultimately, will not be avoided.

So why do we do it?

At first, we choose to live "our truth" instead of *the* truth, because it makes more emotional sense to us. The truth does not seem immediately gratifying. Indeed, it asks us to deny ourselves and put our faith in an invisible Reality. Our truth urges us to seize the day, to make our hopes reality now. We reason we deserve it, and this makes good feelings, if not good sense.

Secondly, we choose to live "our truth" instead of the truth, because the truth is just so darn unfashionable. All the popularly approved people are living their truth. It's the outdated stick-in-the-muds who keep insisting the truth is the real deal. Who wants to be out of the in-crowd?

This is even true for people who find themselves alienated from communities they've always known in order to live "their truth." Many of those who flee evangelicalism cite what living their truth has cost them. One prominent ex-evangelical author and conference speaker who affirms homosexuality and same-sex marriage is prone to citing how many Christians now criticize her and what speaking engagements she's lost. I see her big house, her popular podcast, and her bestselling book on the shelf at Target, and somehow I am not convinced she's lost what was ultimately most important to her.

This "living your truth" stuff is part of the modern creed for the post-evangelical or "progressive evangelical" crowd. But it's not just about liberals affirming popular sins in the name of self-fulfillment. It's also about conservatives affirming political sins in the name of self-exaltation.

Imagine this exchange in the hallway of a conservative evangelical church in November 1992:

Concerned Voter: I don't know. I can't believe the American people elected this man.

Unconcerned Voter: Ah, don't worry. He's a natural leader.

CV: Yes, but some of the things he stands for, some of the things he says are in opposition to the way of Jesus.

UV: He just knows his audience, is all. He says he's a Christian. That's good enough for me.

CV: But does he actually live out what he says he believes? Lots of people are saying he's a womanizer. Or worse.

UV: Who are we to judge? Look, God can use anybody. Think of King David. He was an adulterer too.

Aaaaand scene.

As I said, you have to imagine the above scenario, because I cannot imagine that it actually took place in any conservative church hallway in the early nineties. No, evangelicals stood almost lockstep in opposition to the elected President Bill Clinton that year—and every year after. They did so largely because of his platform, but also because of his questionable character. Indeed, we heard lots and lots and *lots* about his character. Still do, in fact.

Politically minded evangelicals care a lot about character. Except when they don't.

I'm a child of the seventies and eighties. I grew up in the height of Reaganism and the rise of the Moral Majority, Religious Right, and so on. I remember the Sunday Oliver North came to "preach" in our church. I still have the hardback copy of his book that he signed for me, though I don't remember a thing he said from the pulpit. I don't think I'm going out on a limb to suggest that it wasn't a Christ-exalting piece of biblical exposition. I do remember wondering why he was speaking as a patriot when his patriotism seemed to be applied in some kind of scandal.

I don't remember any of the churches I grew up in going overboard on the nationalistic fervor, even during the chilliest years of the latter stages of the Cold War. Patriotism just kinda hung in the background, like the flag on the sides of so many church altars. But, then, the gospel just kinda hung in the background too.

One thing I *do* remember our preachers and Sunday school teachers telling us, however, is how much being a good person mattered. Your reputation, your integrity, your character—this was your currency. This warning was expressed in a variety of contexts and with a variety of applications. It was especially stressed during anxious election seasons, but it was a constant lesson from our elders, for whom personal integrity meant so, so much.

We were schooled on the importance of the Christian worldview— in opposition to postmodernism and other philosophical evils. Our teachers warned us zealously against moral relativism, situational ethics, and hypocrisy.

I was scared into the kingdom by one of those late-seventies *Left Behind*–like films. Nothing could be more important than to stand for the truth, even in the face of the Antichrist's persecution.

We met for See You at the Pole, where evangelical students gathered ostensibly to pray for the country but also, honestly, to thumb their noses at all those worldly humanists who wanted to take away our right to pray in schools.

We ate apologetics books like communion wafers—and were about as nourished. What we learned was to argue, to corner our opponents in their intellectually unfurnished corners, defeating them with our theistic strength and consistency.

And then something happened. The rock-hard truth unchanging became circumstantial application. The pursuit of relevancy fully took over. The pursuit of influence, of power, became more naked. The same figures who denounced Bill Clinton on the grounds of his moral disqualification suddenly found moral relativism a workable strategy in defense of a Republican at least as unqualified. One Christian spokesperson was asked if there was anything the president could do that would endanger his support from evangelical leaders, and he replied flatly, "No."[3]

Another evangelical darling in the lead-up to an election said, "Sometimes you put your Christian values on pause to get the work done."[4]

This is dangerous thinking.

When power becomes your god, you'll do as much biblical gymnastics as it takes to get it or keep it.

Everybody has their own "truth" sitting in the ditch on the road to the real truth, and the master of deflection will be glad to help you rationalize your way to it.

"For the time will come," Paul writes in 2 Timothy 4:3, "when people will not tolerate sound doctrine, but according to their own desires, will multiply teachers for themselves because they have an itch to hear what they want to hear."

We assume this only refers to outright heresy, to the moral relativism of those "out there." But it applies to every kind of relativistic pursuit of truth. The politically idolatrous evangelical dismissing the president's lies or immorality is just as much an ear-scratcher as the health-and-wealth televangelist attempting to spin gospel promises into literal gold.

In this mode, up becomes down if we think it so. Left becomes right, and vice versa. It is an inversion of what God has said is right based on what we think is right. It is like Milton's devil saying, "Evil be thou my Good."[5]

Now that I've had a chance to make everyone angry, let me insist on something I hope we can all agree on: the real truth is not relative. It is not dependent on our desires or our feelings or even our intellectual grasp of it. Truth does not change based on who's in office or on anything that strikes our fancy or convenience.

It is distressing that professing Christians are adopting the kind of moral relativism that has more in common with the rhetorical techniques of opponents to Christianity. Skeptics have been arguing this way for decades in the modern age, as if the demands of progress have rendered the truth claims of the historic faith irrelevant, outdated superstition.

Consider the words of G. K. Chesterton:

> Some dogma, we are told, was credible in the twelfth century, but is not credible in the twentieth. You might as well say that a certain philosophy can be believed on Mondays, but cannot be believed on Tuesdays. You might as well say of a view of the cosmos that it was suitable to half-past three, but not suitable to half-past four. What a man can believe depends upon his philosophy, not upon the clock or the century.[6]

Nor, we might add, upon his interests or opportunities or circumstances.

The truth is that your truth is relative. *The* truth is not.

If God has said something is true, it is true. He doesn't change his mind (Num. 23:19). We are to pass on what we've received (1 Cor. 11:23; 15:3). We are not permitted to change it, twist it, spin it, or even misapply it.

On one level, this is hugely helpful, because we are not at a loss for what God has said and what we're to do with it. The Bible may be a difficult book, but it is mostly difficult in that hard hearts and inverted minds find it difficult to believe and obey. On the things that matter most, it is not difficult to understand.

When we begin to fudge with the Bible's absolute truth claims, we find that we have succumbed to the devil's weighing of our feelings and appetites as greater than God's unchanging standards. But walking by faith in the God who does not change (James 1:17) means, in part, trusting that what is true is ultimately best, even for us, even if we cannot imagine how. Poet and author Jackie Hill Perry put it this way:

> Since God is holy and utterly good by nature, even His harshest commands are worth your obedience. Or to say it another way, if God is as good as He says He is, then every single command is good FOR you even if it doesn't feel good to you.[7]

I find the Sermon on the Mount to be the most frightening portion of Scripture, mainly because as I read it, I begin thinking of all the ways it doesn't apply to me. I immediately start coming up with all the situations where "turn the other cheek" doesn't apply. I think of the circumstances in which "going the second mile" might not be the right thing to do, where "giving to those who ask of you" doesn't mean what it actually says. I want Jesus' kingdom commands to suit my comfortable assumptions and convenient interpretations. And the minute we start doing this is the minute we begin echoing the serpent's "Did God really say . . . ?"

As I said—dangerous.

But to know God is to know him as truthful. This is why the serpent began with that seed of doubt about whether God actually said what he actually said. Satan wants Eve to consider whether she doesn't know God or his truth like she thinks she does, to trade in the certainty of God's words for the relativity of her appetites.

Then, as now, the only antidote to our moral relativism is God's actual words.

THE TRUTH IS WHAT GOD "REALLY SAID"

"I declare the end from the beginning," God said (Isa. 46:10), and while he was more immediately referring to his sovereign foreordination of all things that come to pass, there is relevance here for our understanding of the steadiness and the consistency of what God declares.

There has been some debate of late about the continuity—and discontinuity—between the Old Testament and the New Testament. Didn't God say some things in the Old that he did not say in the New? Are there some laws that are no longer binding?

In a manner of speaking, yes, but we are not left to figure it out on our own. Some will note that the same Old Testament that forbids homosexuality also forbids eating shellfish. We note, then, that in the New Testament, God declares all food clean (Mark 7:19; Acts 10:9–15), while he maintains his forbidding of homosexuality (and all other sexual sin). While it may not be possible to make clean demarcations between the moral law and the so-called ceremonial (or ritual) law—all God's laws are moral laws, really—there appears to be a difference between regulations given to a particular people for a particular time and regulations given for all people in all times.

The point is that we don't have to wonder which is which. The New Testament helps us understand and apply the Old, and we are told which laws do and don't apply to us anymore. The problem isn't really with what we don't understand about God's laws; our real problem is with what we *do* understand about them! We know what he said, and we wish he hadn't said it—at least, not to us.

This is why we've come up with all these loopholes for and caveats about God's laws. It's not about hermeneutics. It's about disobedience. This is why abortion rights advocates rarely talk about the biological science of personhood and instead talk about personal freedoms and autonomy, about "rights."

The entire enterprise of self-orientation erodes boundaries of responsibility and clear outlines of universal truth. The further and further we go into our own sense of experience and perception, the more we begin to question whether there's really a truth at all. There's "my truth" and there's "your truth," but it's possible that ne'er the twain shall meet.

As Pilate washes his hands of the cowardly way he was making a decision by allowing others to make a decision, he also washes his hands of his obligation to what's right.

"You are a king then?" Pilate asked.

"You say that I'm a king," Jesus replied. "I was born for this, and I have come into the world for this: to testify to the truth. Everyone who is of the truth listens to my voice."

"What is truth?" said Pilate. (John 18:37–38)

Jesus pointedly says that people interested in the truth listen to him. Pilate dodges his prisoner's direct truth claims with the same kind of squishy epistemology that rules today.

If you can't win the argument on its own terms, change the terms. Or, better yet, "What really are terms? What is the point of having terms? Maybe term isn't even a real word."

The attempt to redefine reality to suit ourselves is how we've ended up with the sexual chaos today. It's how we've ended up with the wholesale slaughter of upward of 350,000 little girls each year by abortion in the name of "women's rights." It's how we've doggedly (and rightly) protected the innocence of children in their inability to consent to sexual relationships and yet reason they're physically and emotionally mature enough to undergo sex-change operations or take hormones to "change" their gender.

If we cannot acclimate to what we know is true, we'll mess with the nature of knowing itself.

Knowing what God actually said is the only way out of this mess. This is why Jesus said, "Everyone who is of the truth listens to my voice." And it is why we find in Christ's victorious withstanding of temptation in the wilderness an instructive redemption of Eve's succumbing to the serpent's temptation in the garden.

Remember, the devil begins with the nature of knowing God, planting that seed of doubt. "Did God really say . . . ?"

Eve responds with what she remembers God to have said, or at least what she reckons he meant: "We may eat the fruit from the trees in the garden. But about the fruit of the tree in the middle of the garden, God said, 'You must not eat it or touch it, or you will die'" (Gen. 3:2–3).

The devil counters, offering Eve an alternate truth. It is his truth. He suggests she make it her own. Then Eve falls.

Not so Jesus.

I have pointed out previously how the threefold temptation of Eve (and Adam) in Genesis 3 mirrors the threefold temptation of Jesus in the desert. I will say more about this important parallel in our concluding chapter. But for now, notice the difference between Eve's response and Christ's. Notice how after the first satanic parry of Eve's noting what God actually said, she runs out of what God actually said. She either doesn't recall anything pertinent from her Creator about experiencing fulfillment, beauty, and enlightenment in him, or she cares not to bring it up. Jesus, on the other hand, returns every serpentine whisper with a shout of doctrine.

> Then the tempter approached him and said, "If you are the Son of God, tell these stones to become bread."
>
> He answered, "It is written: Man must not live on bread alone but on every word that comes from the mouth of God."
>
> Then the devil took him to the holy city, had him stand on the pinnacle of the temple, and said to him, "If you are the Son of God, throw yourself down. For it is written:
>
> > He will give his angels orders concerning you,
> > and they will support you with their hands
> > so that you will not strike
> > your foot against a stone."

Jesus told him, "It is also written: Do not test the Lord your God."

Again, the devil took him to a very high mountain and showed him all the kingdoms of the world and their splendor. And he said to him, "I will give you all these things if you will fall down and worship me."

Then Jesus told him, "Go away, Satan! For it is written: Worship the Lord your God, and serve only him." (Matt. 4:3–10)

The devil will even resort to twisting the words of Scripture to tempt you away from the truth. But Jesus knows what God *actually* said. In the face of satanic appeal to idolatrous and faithless versions of fulfillment, beauty, and enlightenment, Jesus did not run out of Bible verses.

Eve ran out of Bible verses.

The truth is out there. It is reachable. People of the truth listen to the voice of truth. It doesn't matter what is fashionable to believe, what is expedient to believe, what even *sounds reasonable* to believe—if it defies what God actually said, it is not true. And if it is not true, it is not to be believed.

YOUR FEELINGS ARE REALITY

I struck the board and cried, "No more.
I will abroad.
What, shall I ever sigh and pine?"
—GEORGE HERBERT, "THE COLLAR"

AT ONE POINT IN MY LIFE, I WAS STUCK IN THE upside down of depression. I know well the feeling of not-feeling, as well as that of feeling-too-much. I know what it's like to feel simultaneously like a walking raw nerve and a lump of numbness. It is a perplexing and disorienting existence, which is why most depressed folks cannot find the motivation or energy to do much more than lie around.

How upside down was I? I remember watching my daughters at home when they were probably three and five. I don't remember what happened, but I remember our three-year-old screaming bloody murder about something the five-year-old had done. She wasn't hurt, at least not physically. But she was screaming with streams of tears running down her puffy-pink cheeks and looking to me for comfort. I remember looking at her blankly, unmoved. The memory of this scares me to death, as I am not normally an unemotional person.

During the same time period, I recall losing all sense of rationality over minor mistakes and setbacks. Not being able to get the grass trimmer started drove me to tears. Spilling a drink in the kitchen would spark an inner rage that made me want to pull my hair out.

I am glad to have emerged from those shadows, and while I still experience the occasional bout of melancholy, I've not experienced another time so prolonged and so dark. I am glad to have emerged from that upside-down world unscathed, as my sense of reality was seriously affected. Through a significant portion of that depression, I wrestled with suicidal thoughts and feelings. Psychologists might call what I experienced "suicidal ideation." I did not try to take my own life, but I thought about it and envisioned it constantly, every day and multiple times a day.

I just wanted what I was experiencing to end. I begged God constantly to just "take me." Struggling under the weight of the mess I'd made of my life and the cumulative mess of being me scrambled my sense of reason. I figured if I've hurt so many people, the best thing I can do for them is take myself out of the world.

Depression is like a funhouse mirror. It presents a distorted reflection of one's self. And it becomes increasingly difficult to think what life is like outside the funhouse—or even to believe there *is* a life outside the funhouse.

I once heard a famous pastor talk about his seasons of depression on a speakers' panel at a conference. Another pastor on the panel said, "I have no idea what it feels like to be depressed," and I thought to myself about the second pastor, *I have no idea how you expect to relate to the hurting people in your congregation.* And yet I suspect he sought to relate to them based not on shared experiences but on shared beliefs—that God is real, that God is love, that God is mighty to save.

It's very possible this pastor wasn't very good at empathy. He may not have been the one you wanted in the counseling office or by the hospice bed. But it wouldn't be because he wasn't in touch with the truth. He might not be very good at holding your hand in the midst of your pain, but I bet he could reliably point you to the reality of God.

Thankfully, many pastors are able to do both. That said, the most important thing a pastor can do is *not* validate our feelings, but rather encourage us in the truth. The best pastors remind us that there is deeper and truer reality than what we can at this very moment see, hear, and touch. That doesn't make this world unreal; it just makes it un-ultimate.

And it's not just the depressed who are in danger of having their world defined by their feelings. The weirdos who've never in their lives had a down day are in danger too. An always-positive attitude is no more reflective of reality than an always-negative one.

Yes, how we experience the world matters. At the very least, it tells us something important about ourselves. But how we experience the world doesn't define what is ultimately true.

I know an older man who doesn't know Jesus and yet seems perfectly content in his life. Can you believe that? Of course you can, because you know people just like him. This fellow has a nice family, a nice house, a nice set of friends, a nice savings account, and is himself a genuinely nice guy. When I was growing up in the church and being trained for evangelism, I was constantly told that lost people feel that something is missing in their lives. We all have a God-shaped hole in our hearts, the thinking goes. And this is true. But what is not true is that everybody keenly feels the ache of that void. The truth is, you can be lost and not know it. This man's experience of life does not comport with the reality of his dire need. He is by all spiritual indicators on his way to hell, but he doesn't feel the least bit endangered.

Similarly, you can feel like you're going through hell right now, that all is lost, and yet be perfectly safe in the loving arms of the Father.

The devil loves orchestrating this inversion, where danger feels like safety and safety feels like danger. The apostle Peter says he is "prowling around like a roaring lion, looking for anyone he can devour" (1 Peter 5:8). That word "devour" is informative. The devil isn't out for a nibble. He wants to tear you to shreds and swallow you down his throat.

It makes total sense, then, that Satan would exploit the self-contained rationality of our emotionality. He wants us to define reality according to how we feel, because he knows how overwhelming and all-consuming our feelings can be.

This is why we must stay aware of our feelings without becoming beholden to them.

FEELINGS, SOMETHING MORE THAN FEELINGS

"Facts don't care about your feelings" is one cliché I left unmentioned in the previous chapter's exploration of the lie about "living your truth." It has become a well-worn motto within right-wing pushback against progressive rhetoric on social media. As I write this, "Facts don't care about your feelings" has been posted for three years as conservative pundit Ben Shapiro's pinned tweet on Twitter.

It is true that facts don't care about our feelings. But fact-lovers ought to. Our emotions are like barometers—they reveal the climate of our being. Emotions tell us important things about ourselves and our ability to cope, process, and persevere.

I'll go further: emotions are given to us by God. The all-wise Creator has wired us to feel.

But beginning with the fall of man, we've gotten our wires crossed. The solution, however, is not to disregard the inner workings of ourselves, but to sort them out and manage them according to the wisdom of God—according to reality.

For every single one of us, this is an incredibly complex process and extremely difficult to carry out. Perception is reality for nearly all of us, which is why we find so many challenges to our perceptions not simply jarring but also personally offensive.

To make matters more difficult, many of our emotions are residual from past realities, things that were true that we continue to experience as current truth. This is what makes recovery from trauma so perilous and tender. A victim may be far removed from the very real danger of their past, but they re-experience the offense every day, not as a matter of choice, but as a matter of *wiring*.

Bessel van der Kolk is a medical doctor and professor who specializes in the treatment of trauma. For decades he has studied and cared for patients seeking recovery from abuse or other horrific experiences. In his book *The Body Keeps the Score*, van der Kolk wrote about how trauma, in effect, imprints upon the brain, upon the very physiology of a victim, giving way to a "natural" ease in interpreting experience and intuition as current reality:

> The left brain remembers facts, statistics, and the vocabulary of events. We call on it to explain our experiences and put them in order. The right brain stores memories of sound, touch, smell, and the emotions they evoke. It reacts automatically to voices, facial features, and gestures and places experienced in the past. What it recalls feels like intuitive truth—the way things are.[1]

Van der Kolk's proposed methods for treatment of trauma are somewhat controversial among psychologists, and I personally do not have the authority to endorse or discount them. Certainly, as a Christian, I would want medical treatments and physical therapies to be supplemented with regular rehearsing of biblical truth in the troubled mind. But the research indicating how, for survivors of trauma, "feelings become facts" is compelling and to be ignored only by people who don't care about victims.

Regardless of what you make of van der Kolk's various prescriptions, his diagnoses are incisive. Key treatment strategies involve helping victims experience a rewiring of their realities. This is not accomplished by ignoring their feelings. In fact, part of the process often involves delving further into them, sorting them out one by one in the context of therapy or counseling, in a way "confronting" them. But the goal is not simply to validate one's feelings and therefore live forever a perpetual victim, but rather to methodically bring the reality of one's feelings into the reality of present circumstances. Van der Kolk went on to say, "Simply noticing what you feel fosters emotional regulation, and it helps you to stop trying to ignore what is going on inside you."[2] The goal is to learn how not to be ruled by one's feelings.

As far as I know, Dr. van der Kolk is not a Christian, but this goal is very much aligned with the biblical view of our emotions.

Ignoring your feelings isn't the answer. Facts may not care about your feelings, but Jesus does. Which is why his Word says so much about them.

The point isn't that feelings don't matter or aren't important. The point is that feelings are not the definer of ultimate reality. The Bible points us to think about our feelings, to do the hard work of tuning our disposition to something *more* than feelings.

Think about the kinds of emotional constraints the Word of God puts on those who claim to follow Jesus. "Be angry and do not sin," Paul writes in Ephesians 4:26. "Don't let the sun go down on your anger." In a way, the apostle is affirming anger as a legitimate emotion, a worthy response to all kinds of sin. But being ruled by that anger is itself a sin.

Think also of the fruit of the Spirit in Galatians 5:22–23, which includes qualities like patience, gentleness, and self-control. These are qualities of emotional restraint. The Spirit-led person is not devoid of emotions but also isn't controlled by them. Again, this is not accomplished by ignoring what we feel, but by contemplating what we feel and bringing what we feel into the light of spiritual reality.

In this way we are legitimately angry about injustices of all kinds, and in many cases we may even seek restitution or reparation, especially on behalf of others. But we forego retribution or revenge, because these ignore the spiritual reality that God will take care of the vengeance.

The devil wants us only feeling our feelings, not thinking

about them. His playground is the visible world of experience and reaction. If you start thinking beyond what you see and feel, you might somehow stumble into faith, and he certainly can't have that.

BELIEVING IS SEEING

When Jesus died, his disciples were sad. This was a natural and appropriate emotional response to what they had witnessed. When he suddenly returned from the dead and appeared before them, their sense of reality was seriously being messed with. The sadness was so overwhelming, it threatened to squelch the possibility of joy.

If you recall, Thomas tells the disciples that unless he can touch Jesus' wounds, he will not believe in the resurrection (John 20:25). For Thomas, at least in that moment, seeing was believing.

He gets a bad rap for this, and perhaps deservedly so, but I feel bad for ol' Doubting Thomas. Should he forever be marked by his skepticism? He is just like us. We define our reality according to our senses too.

A week after his declaration of doubt, Thomas is standing before his Lord in the quiet of a locked room. In a profound act of merciful condescension, Jesus invites Thomas to touch his wounds and says, "Because you have seen me, you have believed. Blessed are those who have not seen and yet believe" (John 20:29).

Jesus said a similar thing earlier in his ministry when telling a story of a rich man and a homeless man in the afterlife (Luke 16:19–31). For the whole of his life, the rich man had defined reality according to what he saw. He was content with his riches and all they could buy. He gained the world and lost his soul. The homeless man was named Lazarus, and despite his poverty and pain, he obviously trusted in the reality he could not see, because after he died, he found himself in the very paradise of God.

In Jesus' story, the rich man calls out to Abraham, first for relief, which cannot be supplied. (Remember, if you only live once, you will die twice.) Then he entreats Abraham to send Lazarus back from the dead to his family home to warn them about the dangers of faithless living.

If you can get over the gall of the rich guy still trying to boss the poor guy around even in the afterlife, you must also consider the logic of his request. It makes perfect sense to most people's experience of reality.

"I will believe in Jesus," the unbeliever says, "if I can touch him."

"I will believe in this God stuff," says the atheist, "if he will prove himself to me."

We believe that seeing is believing. If only God would work a miracle in front of us, our definition of reality would change. But we know from experience that even this is not true. People dismiss things they see all the time, especially if their previous belief was exceedingly precious to them. Jesus worked many miracles in front of unbelievers who nevertheless continued on in their unbelief.

"If my unbelieving family witnesses a miraculous resurrection, they will believe," the rich man thinks.

Abraham replies, "If they don't listen to Moses and the prophets, they will not be persuaded if someone rises from the dead" (Luke 16:31).

Well, this is interesting. Jesus is again communicating that belief in what we *don't* see is more important than belief in what we do see. Believing is seeing, in other words.

In fact, according to Jesus, what we hear should be more

defining of our reality than what we see. Specifically, he is refer-ring to what we hear in the Bible. (The phrase "Moses and the prophets" refers to the Scriptures.)

There is a direct line between these episodes and Christ's rebuking of the devil in the desert. Jesus is tempted to give in to his feelings (hunger and fatigue) and believe in what he sees when he is told to turn stones into bread. Instead, he declares that man must not live according to what he feels and sees, but rather by "every word that comes from the mouth of God" (Matt. 4:4).

OUR TOUCHY-FEELY GOD

We dabbled in Job a bit in our exploration of Lie #1, but now I think it is time for a deeper dive. I know many books that deal with the universal experience of human suffering interact with the story of Job, and at the risk of redundancy I do so here for an additionally important reason—namely, Job shows us the experience of a man directly targeted by satanic cruelty.

We learn a lot about the devil in the book of Job, even though he somewhat fades into the background by chapter 3. We learn that he is powerful, that he is cunning, that he is defiant, and that he is entirely subject to the sovereign control of God. This last point may be more or less comforting to you, depending on how you look at it, so it is important for our discussion that we deal with it.

Victor Hugo, author of such revered masterpieces as *Les Misérables* and *The Hunchback of Notre Dame*, once said, "Tomorrow, if all literature was to be destroyed and it was left to me to retain one work only, I should save Job."[3] Anyone who has spent a considerable amount of time in the book may see why. Job is an epic masterpiece itself, one full of Spirit-inspired poetry of unparalleled beauty, theology of unrivaled depth, and pastoral counsel of uncommon grace. Job is simultaneously a poetic treatise on the staggering sovereignty of God and an arm around the hunched shoulders of any person struck down in grief and pain.

And Job is a man who has been struck as low as almost anyone could be struck save Christ himself. And I suppose in the midst of his excruciating grief and pain, Job is not so much concerned that Victor Hugo will save him as he is that God will.

The devil has engineered the death of all of Job's children, the destruction of all of his property, the bankruptcy of all his livelihood, and the affliction of all his bodily health. All the man has left is his miserable life. All Job can do is sit there in the wreckage of his life and wait. For what, he's not quite sure yet.

His friends have shown up. And like most friends of the grieving, they are helpful except when they start trying to be helpful. When we get to chapter 14, Job is responding to his friend Zophar, who has suggested Job's troubles are because of his lack of faith.

Job is a righteous man, we've been told, so he's not *not* thinking about his faith. He knows, satanic attack or not, that nothing happens to him outside the sovereign direction of God. But he's not exactly feeling that, if you know what I mean.

> Since a person's days are determined
> and the number of his months depends on you,
> and since you have set limits he cannot pass,
> look away from him and let him rest
> so that he can enjoy his day like a hired worker.

(JOB 14:5–6)

What's he saying? Basically: "Lay off me! I can't take any more. It's not enough you determine how long we live, God; you also allow hardship to come to us. Can't you just turn your head for a moment and let us have a little freedom?"

The feelings are real. The pain is real. And somehow he knows that although his immediate affliction is at the hands of the devil, he knows the devil is on God's leash. But he is somehow trusting that the hand on that leash *cares*.

This remembrance comes as an exclamatory consolation in "The Collar," a poem from the early seventeenth-century priest George Herbert. The title has perhaps a double meaning, referring both to the clerical collar of those wedded to Christian ministry and to the constraints put on the same by the God they serve. The collar that designates one's commitment also seems a burden, a stricture. Herbert's poem begins as a lament for some unidentified pain. As you read the selections below—and do so slowly, to get the full effect—consider the Job-like torment represented in the cry. See if it does not resonate with any feelings you've ever had, or maybe have right now.

> Sure there was wine
> Before my sighs did dry it; there was corn
> Before my tears did drown it.
> Is the year only lost to me?
> Have I no bays to crown it,
> No flowers, no garlands gay? All blasted?
> All wasted? . . .
> Away! take heed;
> I will abroad.
> Call in thy death's-head there; tie up thy fears;

He that forbears
To suit and serve his need
Deserves his load."
But as I raved and grew more fierce and wild
At every word,
Methought I heard one calling, *Child!*
And I replied *My Lord*.[4]

In the end, what consoles the lamenter is not a removal of pain or circumstances. Rather, he hears God calling him "child." And he knows God not simply as a sovereign designer of his woes, but as a loving father who cares. That is enough, strange as it may sound to many.

Earlier in the book of Job, when Job's wife suggests he curse God and die (2:9), Job thinks, "Should we accept only good from God and not adversity?" (2:10). Many of us find our theology closer at hand in the onset of pain. It is when the pain prolongs that we begin to wrestle with it.

I think of the depressed person of Psalm 42, attributing all the "breakers and waves" crashing over him to the hand of God as well. He is caught between sound doctrine and devastating grief. The longer it goes, the more opportunities for doubt to creep in.

"You've got my attention, and I've learned my lesson," we cry out to God. Still the darkness remains.

Does God not care? Is he a cosmic sadist?

What happens to our emotional well-being when our theology of God's lovingkindness crashes into the harsh wall of reality?

The bulk of the book of Job consists of the divine dialogue of prayer. Job speaks to God. God speaks to Job. That this is a reality is itself infinitely helpful and comforting. We may not have a God who will keep us away from all experiences of pain and suffering, but we have a God who listens and speaks. He is not indifferent.

What he says is important, however, and the astute reader notices that God never "poor babys" Job. Instead he whisks him into a dizzying panorama of his own glory and sovereign power. So much of what he shows Job are things Job cannot see, at least not in the moment. "Were you there, Job, when I created sea monsters?" That's just one of the strange things God says to our sufferer (41:1).

Of course Job wasn't there for that. He may not have ever seen a Leviathan, much less its creation. He hasn't seen nearly any of the things God puts in front of his troubled mind to ponder. Why would God go about comforting Job this way? He is proving himself anything but touchy-feely.

When we are suffering, we long for a touchy-feely God. And in his incarnation, the Son of God has come to touch and to feel. Not only is God not indifferent, he is able to sympathize with our weaknesses (Heb. 4:15). But the touchy-feely God isn't exactly what we need. What God has come to do with his beloved servant Job is remind him of the deeper reality in play, the bigger story that will make his pain—while perhaps not bearable, perhaps not explicable—*meaningful*.

The Lord has allowed the satanic crushing of Job in order to show him the reality of what he could not lose.

WHAT JOB HAD LEFT

This is what Job sees: sorrow, loss, sickness, a hurtful spouse, and unhelpful friends. He begins to note the apparent futility of it all. He feels hopeless.

> There is hope for a tree:
> If it is cut down, it will sprout again,
> and its shoots will not die.
> If its roots grow old in the ground
> and its stump starts to die in the soil,
> the scent of water makes it thrive
> and produce twigs like a sapling.
> But a person dies and fades away;
> he breathes his last—where is he?
> As water disappears from a lake
> and a river becomes parched and dry,
> so people lie down never to rise again.
>
> (14:7–12)

You can see the tree's fruit. It bounces back. All we see of a person, though, is getting old, dying, and wasting away. That's what we can *see*. That's the reality we feel. This is the reality Satan wants us to feel.

When I was mired in my own depressive season, I felt distilled down to a fine point and utterly alone. Even with people around me, people who professed to love me, I could not shake the weighty grief of loneliness. *Nobody understands*, I thought. *Nobody cares*, I believed. *This is pointless.*

Job is there:

> But as a mountain collapses and crumbles
> and a rock is dislodged from its place,
> as water wears away stones
> and torrents wash away the soil from the land,
> so you destroy a man's hope.

81

You completely overpower him, and he passes on;
you change his appearance and send him away.
If his sons receive honor, he does not know it;
if they become insignificant, he is unaware of it.
He feels only the pain of his own body
and mourns only for himself.

(14:18–22)

Job has been stripped down to his essence. All his comforts are gone. All his physical pleasures are gone. All his material goods are gone. All his earthly joys are gone. What is he left with? "Only the pain of his own body."

He is left with only pain. But also . . . hope. Maybe one reason God allowed this attack was so that Job would learn not to trust in what he sees but instead to snuggle up close to God.

In my days as a pastor, I would often find myself sitting across from people overcome with hurt. The most common question they all wanted answered was "Why?"

"Why had God allowed this? Why is God doing this to me?"

As the designated religious professional, it was expected that I might have an answer to that question. As it pertains to people's specific trials and tribulations, I did not. But I would ask a question of my own, and it usually went something like this: "If you weren't going through this, would you be as close to God as you are right now?"

In all my years of asking that question, I never heard anyone say, "Yes."

This is a difficult truth to accept, but the Lord is always more interested in deepening our sense of need for him than he is in giving us reasons not to need him at all.

And this is where Job is. Everything he sees—touches, smells, hears, *feels*—is miserable. His life *looks* hopeless. And yet—God bless him—despite his visible tragedy, Job decides that if pain is all he has left, he might as well have it with some hope on the side.

I think of the deathbed words of Aragorn, High King of Gondor, as recorded in an appendix to Tolkien's *The Return of the King*: "In sorrow we must go, but not in despair. Behold! we are not bound for ever to the circles of the world, and beyond them is more than memory, Farewell!"[5]

Depression, perhaps, yes. But not despair.

See, Christians don't hope as the world hopes. When the world hopes, they are engaging in wishful thinking. "I *hope* this or that happens," they think. They think that when a man dies, as Job says, he just fades away; he breathes his last. "You only live once." That's it. That's all they can see.

But Christian hope is not like that. It defies what we can see and it is ripe with the promise of what cannot be seen.

- "You will not grieve like the rest, who have no hope."—1 Thessalonians 4:13
- "And our hope for you is firm, because we know that as you share in the sufferings, so you will also share in the comfort."—2 Corinthians 1:7
- ". . . because of the hope reserved for you in heaven." —Colossians 1:5
- "Christ in you, the hope of glory."—Colossians 1:27
- "Christ Jesus *is* our hope."—1 Timothy 1:1 (emphasis added)
- "We have this hope as an anchor for the soul, firm and secure . . ."—Hebrews 6:19

- "Now faith is the *reality* of what is hoped for, the proof of what is not seen."—Hebrews 11:1 (emphasis added)

See, the world's hope is hollow. The believer's hope is firm. Because the believer's hope is Jesus! And just because you can't see him doesn't mean he's not real. Just because you don't see him now, doesn't mean you won't see him then.

Satan wants you to believe that you are all alone, that when you are stripped down to your essence and left with only pain, that's all you have. He does not want you to see the reality that Jesus will never leave you or abandon you (Heb. 13:5), that he will be with us all the way to the end (Matt. 28:20).

After everything was stolen, what Job had left was hope. And hope, properly placed, is one thing the devil can't take.

HOPE DEFIES WHAT WE FEEL AND DEMANDS WHAT WE DON'T

When you get to the end of your rope, there is Jesus. This is grounds for immense confidence, even as life threatens to undo us. Even as the condemnation from our Accuser roars in our ears, the surety of Christ's possession of us and our possession of him is something not even the supernatural power of Satan can assail.

Therefore, hope defies what is seen. Everything may look bleak, our reality may be that we feel that all is lost, but if we have Christ, we defy what is visible. And we cling to hope, which demands what is invisible.

By "demand," I don't mean hope demands things of God. We are in a place to make requests of our Father, but not to order him around. I only mean that hope is a calling for what lies beyond. Hope demands things of *us*, really—that we will not assume that what we see is all there is to the story.

So Job prays:

> If only you would hide me in Sheol
> and conceal me until your anger passes.
> If only you would appoint a time for me
> and then remember me.
> When a person dies, will he come back to life?
> If so, I would wait all the days of my struggle
> until my relief comes.
>
> (14:13–14)

Job is saying, in essence, "My hope is that this will be worth it." He's not saying, "Oh, I *hope* this is worth it." He's saying, "My hope is that I *know* this will be worth it." So even if he can't see through the tears of his pain, he knows he can endure given the end that's coming.

"When a person dies, will he come back to life?" This is the first hint of where Job's ultimate hope lies.

"I would wait all the days of my struggle until my relief comes."

Let me make it personal. Let me ask you this: If you are going through something incredibly painful right now—what in your mind would make it "worth it"? Maybe it's simply deliverance from the circumstances, relief from the pain. Maybe, in your mind, nothing is worth what you're going through.

But if you believe in the sovereignty of God, and that, therefore, he has somehow, for whatever reason you don't see, allowed this trial to come into your life—can you at least believe that he means it ultimately for your good?

Because whatever you brought into your mind when I asked the question "What would make this worth it?" reveals where your hope is found. Is your hope found in what you see? If so, you *should* probably feel hopeless all the time.

Paul writes in Romans 8:24–25: "Hope that is seen is not hope, because who hopes for what he sees? Now if we hope for what we do not see, we eagerly wait for it with patience."

In his parable about the afterlife called *The Great Divorce*, C. S. Lewis put it this way through the words of his imagined guide, George MacDonald:

> That is what mortals misunderstand. They say of some temporal suffering, "No future bliss can make up for it," not knowing that Heaven, once attained, will work backwards and turn even that agony into a glory.[6]

This is what Job is doing at this moment. His hope is demanding what is unseen. He is committing to eagerly waiting, to enduring. We could hear him in Job 14:14 this way: "If I could know I'm going to come back to life—that *this* isn't all there is—I will endure this struggle till that day comes. If that's what it takes, Lord, I will do it."

What about you? If you knew this life isn't all there is, how would it affect how you live today? This week? How would it affect your hope in the midst of suffering?

Lottie Moon was a Baptist missionary to China in the late nineteenth to early twentieth centuries. She served for forty years, largely in the Shandong Province, enduring numerous hardships along the way. She was roundly hated by her mission field, having earned the nickname "devil woman." Moon once wrote that she knew she would be murdered if those who designed to do so had the opportunity.

On top of that, acclimating to the culture was slow going for her, and she struggled to learn Mandarin Chinese. Her sister's deteriorating health was a constant source of worry. Her missionary supervisor was also in dire straits mentally and emotionally. Moon found herself in the midst of feuding local missionaries, constantly trying to broker peace between those who ought to have been working together. As she got older, Moon began to suffer from some mental health issues of her own, it seems.

And she did all of this as a single woman. Can you imagine the pain, the fear, the loneliness?

While you may not be able to identify with her mission to China, perhaps you can identify with a love unfulfilled. We learn that she fell in love with a seminary professor. He was a bit older, and we don't have a lot of details about their relationship, only that the feeling was mutual. And yet it was never fulfilled.

There were perhaps theological differences between them, as her suitor eventually adopted Unitarianism. Maybe it was a vocational divide: she desiring to serve overseas, he desiring to stay home. In any event, we know that on top of all her physical and spiritual suffering, Lottie Moon experienced one of the most common struggles for single (and even many married) persons— unfulfilled romantic desires.

"God had first claim on my life," she said, "and since the two conflicted, there could be no question about the result."[7]

Lottie Moon did not have an easy lot in life. But her hope

was not in her feelings or her circumstances. She knew the most important thing about her was settled, and this in turn helped to settle her heart.

Hope defies what is seen, and hope demands what is unseen.

HOPE WILL BE REALIZED

When the serpent proffered the forbidden fruit to Eve, he was tempting her to hope for things she already had *as if she didn't have them*. There is no greater fulfillment, beauty, and enlightenment than that found in communion with God. The devil promised her those things in the one way that would fail to deliver them!

Job, then, is toiling away on the cursed side of the fall. He can compound his pain by pursuing the devilish way out of it—seeking relief only where it *isn't*—or he can wait with hope, trusting in the deliverance yet to come.

On this side of Christ's first coming, we can look back on what Job was looking forward to. And yet, like Job, we still look forward to the consummation of what Jesus has inaugurated in his first-century ministry.

When Job looks forward to the end, this is his first hope:

> You would call, and I would answer you.
> You would long for the work of your hands.
> For then you would count my steps
> but would not take note of my sin.
> My rebellion would be sealed up in a bag,
> and you would cover over my iniquity.
>
> (14:15–17)

Even from the dim vantage point of antiquity, ages before Christ's birth, what Job ultimately longs for is not temporary comfort but eternal life. That his sin would not be noted. That his rebellion would be vanquished. That his unrighteousness would be covered.

Believe it or not, Job's hope is in the good news of Jesus Christ.

Job is himself a pre-figure of Jesus, the man who was the Son of God incarnate, taking on flesh in our broken world in order to suffer. Unlike Job, Jesus knew what he was getting himself into. He was willing to be afflicted (Luke 22:42). So he went willingly to the cross and endured its shame, its torture, its death—for us.

And after all seemed lost, after the darkest of days, after the feelings of grief and fear threatened to become reality forever, there is a thrill of hope. The resurrection.

To put our faith in Jesus, then, is to cling to the one who has latched himself to us in the deepest, most seriously eternal love ever to be known. The Lord of the universe so unites us to himself that his death becomes ours, his resurrection becomes ours, and no matter where we are, in health or in pain, in happiness or in grief, in riches or in poverty, in certainty or in confusion, we are hidden with him in God himself (Col. 3:3).

To turn your back on him, to put your faith in only what you see now, is to decide not to see him later. Instead, it is to choose the death that comes after death, the wages of our sin, which is eternal condemnation in hell. The one who holds hands with Jesus, however, has an eternal joy to look forward to.

If you're a Christian, the most important thing about your life—your eternal destiny—is settled. "This hope will not disappoint us, because God's love has been poured out in our hearts through the Holy Spirit who was given to us" (Rom. 5:5).

This hope will not disappoint us. This hope, as some other translations put it, "does not put us to shame" (ESV, NIV).

I want you to put yourself in the sandals of a Jewish man or woman in the last days of the year 1 BC. You don't know it's 1 BC, of course! You only know it's been four hundred years since Malachi. It's been four hundred years since God has spoken through his prophets. And you're tired. You're oppressed. You long for comfort, for deliverance, for justice. And the hope for God to do anything about any of it is starting to feel like an urban legend. *If he's up there,* you begin to think, *he doesn't care about us.*

Picture a couple of shepherds in very late 1 BC. They're just watching the sheep under the stars, as they have for years, maybe decades. And two guys, buddies, lean against a boulder, watching their flocks. Two months earlier they were leaning against that same rock, like they had so many times before, and one shepherd says to the other, "Hey, Ernie." (Let's pretend his name is Ernie.)

Ernie says, "Yeah?"

"Do you ever sit and think to yourself if any of that Messiah stuff is true?"

"What do you mean?"

"I mean, my grandpa used to recite to me all the Scriptures he knew. Isaiah. Jeremiah. Job. I've never forgotten them. And when I was younger I used to really believe them. But now, sometimes I wonder . . . I mean, was it all just fairy tales?"

"What are you talking about, fairy tales?" Ernie says. "Of course not. The Lord God himself inspired those prophecies."

"I know, I know. But it's been, like, four hundred years since the last prophet. The Romans own everything. Our preachers are mean. Our activists get crucified. If God was ever speaking, he sure doesn't seem to be speaking today. He's been silent a long time, since long before you and I were born. And day after day, night after night, we come out here and we stare at these stars, and we assume there's a heaven up there, and we assume there's a God up there doing something. But if there is, he has a funny way of showing it. You never think to yourself, what if *this is it*? Like, what if this is all there is?"

And Ernie says, "Man, that's life. Life is just waiting. For who knows how long. Maybe another four hundred years, I don't know. But I know God's up there somewhere. I know he's all around here somewhere. And just 'cause we can't see him, and just 'cause it looks like he's done talking, doesn't mean it's so. Look up at that sky."

And his friend—we'll call him Ralph—looks up.

"One day, my man," Ernie continues. "One day, he's gonna split that sky in two and come right down here and set everything back the way he wanted it."

Ralph looks up at those stars. "Man, I hope so."

Months go by. The shepherds are out with their sheep. Just as they've been doing for years. It's Christmas night, but they don't know that. Christmas doesn't exist yet. To them, it's just one more night, same as all the others. Same ol', same ol'. Nothing ever changes.

And Ernie and Ralph are leaning against that rock again, in silence. And they're looking up at the stars.

And for a second, it looks like one star seems to twinkle a little brighter. And—is that possible?—it looks like it's getting bigger. Ralph rubs his eyes, looks back up.

Yeah, it's definitely getting bigger. Maybe even closer.

And then over the field, the light gets brighter and brighter, until it's almost like daytime. And then it seems like the whole place is on fire, except nobody's getting hurt. And all the shepherds are freaking out, terrified. They're falling on the ground, trembling in fear. It's like an invasion is afoot.

And suddenly a figure comes walking out of the blaze. An angel has come down. He says, "I proclaim to you good news of great joy that will be for all the people: today in the city of David a Savior was born for you, who is the Messiah, the Lord."

Can you imagine?

What was it that Job could look forward to? *Maybe* he had a hope that he would get his fortune and health back. We do know that at the end of the story, he has all those things restored. But he can't get his kids back. And in any event, he doesn't *know* that's going to happen. Certainly he never presumes. For all he knows, this is it. This is the end. Broken, defeated, grief-stricken, and shot through with agony. This is what his life is always going to be like. It couldn't get worse. And then it does. And it certainly can't seem to get better.

All along, we never see Job say, "I hope I get my stuff back." No, where is his hope? A few chapters later, he says this:

> But I *know* that my Redeemer lives
> and at the end he will stand on the dust.
> Even after my skin has been destroyed
> yet I will see God in my flesh.
> I will see him myself;
> my eyes will look at him, and not as a stranger.
> My heart longs within me.
>
> (JOB 19:25–27, EMPHASIS ADDED)

This is Job's hope: first, that the Lord would not take note of his sin, and then, because of that, that the Lord would deliver on the promise of hope, that he would actually know God personally forever. "Lord, I don't know what you're doing, and I don't know the ins and outs of your providentially orchestrating this smoking crater that is my life, but I do know this: when it's all said and done, I will look you in the face and see into your eyes and, whether I understand or not, I will see you, and you will see me, and all will be well."

"My heart longs within me," Job cries in worshipful hope, and I hear in this lament the foreshadow of Peter's declared fulfillment, "Blessed be the God and Father of our Lord Jesus Christ. Because of his great mercy he has given us new birth into a living hope through the resurrection of Jesus Christ from the dead" (1 Peter 1:3). It is this kind of hope that prompts Job to say to God elsewhere, in essence, "Even if you kill me, I will hope in you" (Job 13:15).

I don't know where your reading of this chapter finds you at the moment. Maybe you're desperate right now for that thrill of hope.

We seem to forget that when the wise men came to see the Christ child in Bethlehem, a village of about fifteen hundred people, because of Herod's decree that every boy under the age of two be slaughtered, there were at least a dozen, perhaps up to twenty or more families, in the immediately surrounding areas mourning the murder of their babies. That's the dark, grief-stricken, hopeless world Jesus was born into.

And the way the Bible forecasts the second coming of our Lord, we see that it will be preceded by a great time of tribulation unlike anything ever seen (Matt. 24; 2 Thess. 2:1–12; Rev. 7). As far as the Lord's timing is concerned, it seems like the cliché is not a cliché—it's always darkest before the dawn.

So what are we to do?

> Do not think of following Christ into glory, unless you go
> through the press here. Look forward, my brethren, into eter-
> nity and behold Christ coming and his reward with him, to
> give a kind recompense for all the temptations and difficulties
> of this present life.[8]

Whatever you're going through, it will be worth it. You can
endure with hope, because Christ has come to be born, live, die,
and rise again. He is here in Spirit now. And he will come again.

Doesn't this make it all worth it?

The forbidden fruit cannot deliver. This is one reason why it
is forbidden. But hope that defies what is seen, hope that demands
what is unseen will deliver on what has been promised.

What you feel is not reality. That is at best a half-truth, at
worst a lie. And in any event, whatever you feel is not as real as
the One you hope for.

You'll see.

LIE #5

YOUR LIFE IS WHAT
YOU MAKE IT

It is my duty, said he, to distrust mine own ability, that
I may have reliance on him that is stronger than all.
—JOHN BUNYAN, *THE PILGRIM'S PROGRESS*

IN JULY 2018, THE *NEW YORK DAILY NEWS* PROMOTED
an article about Kylie Jenner with the copy, "19-year-old Kylie
Jenner is worth $900 million and on pace to become the youngest
self-made billionaire ever. What are you doing with your life?"

If you don't know who Kylie Jenner is, do not fret, for I shall
tell you. She is one of the younger sisters of Kim Kardashian, who
is no entrepreneurial slouch herself. Kylie and Kim share a mother
in Kris Jenner, though Kim's father is the late celebrity lawyer
Robert Kardashian (most famous recently from the O. J. Simpson
murder trial) and Kylie's father is the transgendered Caitlyn

Jenner, formerly known as Bruce Jenner. The whole Kardashian enterprise toward mega-riches was precipitated by the rise of their VH1 "reality" television show, *Keeping Up with the Kardashians*, which itself was really precipitated by Kim Kardashian's leaked sex tape.

From sex tape to reality show, the Kardashians have parlayed this famous-for-being-famous strategy into modeling gigs, clothing labels, fragrance lines, and more. While I'm sure there is a lot of business acumen—and certainly a lot of marketing savvy—at work in the accumulation of $900 million, when I think of "self-made," I tend to think of the small-business owner making things, building things, crafting things. Tangible products or services that add money not just to his pocket but to others' as well, that maybe even contribute something of value to the experience of daily life and work.

The pursuit of the American dream has been the hotbed for countless heartwarming tales of people pulling themselves up by their bootstraps out of poverty. When I think "self-made millionaire," I tend to think rags to riches, not sex tape to reality show.

But it's the question in the article promo that really gets me: "What are you doing with your life?" First, the implication is that if I'm not actively working my way toward billionaire status, I must be wasting my life. As far as ads go, the use of shame is a unique technique in our day of safe speech and safe spaces.

Second, however, the standard for our shaming is utterly modern. What exactly does Kylie Jenner *do*? We've seen wealthy heiresses and princesses before, young women who do nothing but laze about and spend the family's money, but Jenner, remember, is "self-made." If she is the model for what I should be doing with my life, I'm curious what trajectory my life should be taking.

What are my steps to $900 million? Why exactly is she a model for financial success?

I read the article.[1] Kylie oversees the cosmetics line that bears her name. It is operated out of her mother's house with just seven employees. This business accounts for $800 million of her fortune.

What does Kylie Jenner do? Well, she makes money hand over fist parlaying her sister's immorality and her family's vacuity into persuading young women to buy sweatshop makeup in order to identify with the Kardashian image.

Or maybe it's just good, cheap makeup; I don't know.

What I do know is that I'll be darned if I'm gonna be shamed into feeling like a failure because my life (or my pocketbook) doesn't resemble Kylie Jenner's.

The holding up of Kylie Jenner as a model for "what you should do with your life" represents nearly everything dysfunctional about America's moral and spiritual life.

"Famous for being famous" is a distinctly modern, distinctly Western phenomenon. Perhaps it began with the reality TV era. But it has become a bona fide aspiration within the American dream. When you asked most school-aged children of my generation what we wanted to be when we grew up, most of the answers would run along the lines of doctor, teacher, policeman, nurse. Maybe the occasional baseball player. Today, the answers seem to be dominated by the likes of rap or pop star, athlete, actor, or—most confounding of all—YouTube star.

To be clear, I am not saying there's anything inherently wrong with any of those professions. But the fact that these have become the most popular childhood aspirations tells us something about the culture our kids are growing up in. It tells us something important about what they see *us*—their guardians, their guides—most valuing.

There may be only one twentysomething female billionaire, but there are literally thousands of young women on social media trying to emulate the Kardashian aesthetic and ethos. I recently read about the trend of faux sponsorships on Instagram, in which people pretend to be featuring certain products (like handbags or even trips to luxury hotels), when really those things are just procured on their own dimes. We used to turn our noses up at people trying to pass off paid content as real life. Now just the *illusion* of being bought is itself a status symbol. The idea is that if I can convince you that somebody gave me money to hype their product, you will think I'm somebody important.

Since the fall of mankind, every culture has fallen for its own version of the lie that "the world is what you make it." Today I am pressed to ask the deeper question, "Is *what* we're making of this world worth it?"

MAKING A DEAL WITH THE DEVIL

Mo money, mo problems. It's not just a Biggie lyric. It's a Christian principle.

The Bible does not speak of wealth as a sin, but it does speak of wealth as a very spiritually precarious possession. Jesus himself spoke over and over again about the difficulties faced by the rich in entering the kingdom. This is perhaps best exemplified in the exchange with the rich young ruler (Matt. 19), who went away sad after Jesus told him to sell all his possessions and give them to the poor. We would be wrong to extrapolate from this episode that people shouldn't be rich, but we would be right to extrapolate from it that if anything takes the place of Christ as treasure in our hearts, we ought to cut it out, no matter the bleeding.

The sense of power that comes with accumulation is as old as accumulation. Solomon pondered it in Ecclesiastes, warning all who read that chasing wealth is like chasing the wind. Is that what you want to do with your life?

"I think everybody should get rich and famous and do everything they ever dreamed of so they can see that it's not the answer." This line is often attributed to Jim Carrey, derived perhaps from similar thoughts he shared in an interview promoting one of his movies.[2] Carrey's not the first to suggest such things, and yet we never believe them. It almost seems like the more you make, the less you really have.

So if we won't believe God on this subject and we won't even believe rich and famous people who've been there, done that, who do we believe?

Again, the devil took him to a very high mountain and showed him all the kingdoms of the world and their splendor. And he said to him, "I will give you all these things if you will fall down and worship me." (Matt. 4:8–9)

Here we find the biblical inspiration for the traditional mythic tale of making a pact with the devil. Perhaps the artistic heritage of these perennial stories begins with the Faust legend from the German Renaissance in the late fifteenth century. First popularized in Christopher Marlowe's *The Tragical History of Doctor Faustus* and remythologized over and over in subsequent comedic morality plays, the story follows Faust as he makes a business deal with the devil. He will "sell his soul" in exchange for the devil's servitude for twenty-four years.

We've had many updated variations on the Faust legend. One of the best known from the heart of Americana is the Southern folktale from the early twentieth century about the (very real) blues guitarist Robert Johnson. It is said that at the crossroads near Dockery Plantation in Mississippi he sold his soul to the devil in exchange for being a great musician. The legend is so bound up with the Johnson bio, it has earned its own multiparagraph history on Johnson's Wikipedia page and has inspired countless derivations including an allusion in the Coen Brothers' film *O Brother, Where Art Thou?*, a country and western adaptation in Charlie Daniels's song "The Devil Went Down to Georgia," and a weird eighties retelling in the Ralph Macchio vehicle simply titled *Crossroads*.

What is interesting about so many of the retellings is how they end. In the original legend, Faust spends his twenty-four years living it up with wine, women, and song. He gets rich, he gets powerful, he gets *experienced*. And when the pact hits the deadline, a devastated Faust warns his friends and family to repent and make better use of their time before the devil comes to claim what's his. The story typically ends with Faust's body spread gorily all over his bedroom and his soul tormented in the fires of hell.

In the modern retellings, the devil always seems to get bested. When Johnny rosins up his bow in Charlie Daniels's song, he is on his way to out-fiddling Satan. Even Ralph Macchio somehow outplays the devil's guitarist in *Crossroads*, played by legendary rock-and-roll axman Steve Vai—which is about as unlikely as Macchio winning all those fights in the Karate Kid series.

Do you notice what has happened? We've somehow changed the moral of this entire genre of stories. The moral used to be

"Don't make a deal with the devil, because no amount of worldly gain is worth your soul." Now the moral appears to be "Go ahead and fraternize with the devil, because you're smarter and stronger than him."

That's how stupid we are. And it's how stupid the accumulation of stuff—be it possessions, money, or simply fame or success—can make us, if we're not careful.

It is a lot like drunkenness. Many men find their sense of invincibility is enhanced when they become intoxicated. Everything is exaggerated, including the ego. They feel and act bigger than they are. But they are actually slower, dumber, and more vulnerable.

Money, fame, and stuff are like that. The more we have, the more secure we may feel, but if the Bible is to be believed, the more spiritually vulnerable we actually are. It's as though we've become drunk.

Look, the devil is very good at what he does. He would not continually make the same offer of worldly gain for millennia if it didn't work. He knows it does. Over and over again, it does. He wants you to see $900 million in the hands of a do-nothing celebutante and feel ashamed of yourself, and envious too. He wants you to hold your soul cheap and the stuff of this world precious. He wants you to make the bargain.

He even wants you to think you're too smart to fall for the trick. He wants you to think you're too powerful. He likes his prey to swagger before he destroys them.

GOD IS NOT HOLDING OUT ON YOU

When the serpent tempted Eve with a promise of fulfillment, beauty, and enlightenment, he was in essence suggesting that God forbade the fruit because he wanted to keep those blessings to himself. The implied truth claim from Satan is this: "God is holding out on you."

Therefore, the logic goes, you should get what you can while you can, because if you're going to make it in this world, it will be by your own hand. The world God made is not good, the lie goes. If you want a world that satisfies your deepest longings, you'll have to make it yourself.

I wonder how many people on their deathbed regret not pursuing more money or physical pleasure. I bet some do, actually. Maybe many. If you're thinking you're about to enter a great void of nonexistence, you may have some regrets about not sleeping with your secretary when you had a chance or making that gambling trip out to Las Vegas. We like to think that dying people only regret not mending relational fences or not spending enough time with their kids, but a lot of people hold their souls really cheap even when it's time to turn them in.

Once I shared the good news of Jesus with a man dying of cancer. He had maybe a week or two to live. I explained that Christ's grace could cover a lifetime of rejecting him if only, by faith, the dying man would reach out for him in that moment. If he would repent of his sin and trust in Jesus, he would be given eternal life. "Nope," he said. He wasn't interested. He explained that he'd made it through his whole life thus far without believing in Jesus, so he saw no point in doing it now.

There lay the self-made man, skeletal and wheezing in a hospital bed, shaking his brittle fist at the God who made him up until his final breath.

I've shared the good news of grace with numerous people in the context of dying. Some were on their deathbeds, some were next to a loved one's deathbed, and many were at funerals after a loved one had passed. My instinct is that the context would heighten the sensitivity to a gospel announcement, that people might even be willing to "take a chance," given the stakes so readily visible.

Instead, I've noticed a fair amount of skepticism and indifference. I theorize that it's the sheer incomprehensibility of grace that may trip people up. There's stubbornness, sure, like the man I just mentioned, who apparently saw no benefit in breaking his long-standing tradition of faithlessness. But there are some who— pondering the idea that a holy God would forgive a lifetime of sin and toss them an *eternal* lifeline in exchange for a few hours, days, weeks of timid faith—find the whole thing simply too ludicrous to believe. There has to be a catch, they think. And whatever it is, they're not falling for it. We will not trust someone if we think they're not telling us the whole truth, if we suspect they're holding out on us.

Pondering the subject of death and dying, the Puritan Richard Baxter wrote, "I fear a *distrust* of God and my Redeemer has had too great a hand in my desires."[3]

> Did God really say, "You can't eat from any tree in the garden"? . . . In fact, God knows that when you eat it your eyes will be opened and you will be like God, knowing good and evil. (Gen. 3:1, 5)

The catch is Satan's. You gain "opened eyes," but you lose your soul.

What has been unleashed through the Edenic catastrophe is the encoding in our spiritual DNA of an irrational distrust in the Creator and a rationalized worship of self.

"You will be like God." This is what we chase when we pursue what we believe God has held back from us. It is an attempt to achieve justice against an unjust God and, thus, fashion ourselves as judges of him. It is, plainly, idolatry.

What the devil offered Eve—who was already queen of the world!—was an enthronement of herself over and against God himself. "All that God has given you is not quite enough, is it?" he hissed. "There's more to have, you know. He wants to keep from you what only he has. What a stingy God. What a miser. He doesn't want to share his deity with you. Well, you can show him. He's given you a will, so why not use it? The fruit is right here for the taking. Why would he put it right here if he didn't want you to have it? There's no holding you back now. Let's see what you guys can make of the world without these terrible restraints."

MAKING YOUR OWN LIFE IS TREASONOUS

"Your life is what you make it" is the same lie as "you will be like God."

We see what a disaster this approach to life in a fallen world brings from the moment Adam and Eve eat the forbidden fruit. They thought they'd be God-like, experiencing an upgrade to their creatureliness, and instead their creatureliness is warped. With visions of absolute power in their heads, they instead find themselves sweating while working a hard and thorny ground. Definitely not God-like.

The closest thing we had to creating life ourselves, conceiving and bearing children, now becomes a painful ordeal.

The firstborn son Cain does resemble the fickle gods of

paganism, overcome with resentment and spite, murdering his brother in a jealous rage.

The civilization that rises from the ashes of the fall becomes so corrupt that God makes an example of it. "You are not gods. I AM." And in saving one family, he washes the slate clean in a judgmental flood.

The civilization that rises from the waters of the flood is so corrupt, they make an example of themselves. They make a tower to heaven for the fame of their own name (Gen. 11:4). It is a monolithic tribute to the self. To this point, it is mankind's grandest achievement, a monument to the power and might of self-made men everywhere.

God "comes down" to look at it (Gen. 11:5).

Seen from the perspective of the true kingdom of God, all of mankind's self-deifying bluster appears so, so wimpy. In his poem "Ye Shall Be Gods," borrowing of course from Genesis 3, as well as Psalm 82:6 and John 10:34, Oscar Wilde posits man's rise from the postlapsarian ruins to self-willed coronation. An excerpt:

> The spirit of man is arisen
> And crowned as a mighty King.
> The people have broken from prison
> And the voices once voiceless now sing.
> Cry aloud, O dethroned and defeated,
> Cry aloud for the fading of might,
> Too long were ye feared and entreated,
> Too long did men worship thy light.[4]

The one dethroned, by the way, is the Creator. The tables have turned in Wilde's revisionist history. The judged has become the judge, and God has become defeated. The poem is satanic. But not just because of its inversion of explicit references to Creator and creature. It is satanic in the way it deifies the creature, makes him (or her) a god.

Similarly, consider William Ernest Henley's "Invictus":

> Out of the night that covers me,
> Black as the pit from pole to pole,
> I thank whatever gods may be
> For my unconquerable soul.
> In the fell clutch of circumstance
> I have not winced nor cried aloud.
> Under the bludgeoning of chance
> My head is bloody, but unbowed.
> Beyond this place of wrath and tears
> Looms but the Horror of the shade,
> And yet the menace of the years
> Finds and shall find me unafraid.
> It matters not how strait the gate,
> How charged with punishments the scroll,
> I am the master of my fate,
> I am the captain of my soul.[5]

I am sorry for all the poetry in this chapter, but I did spot you Kylie Jenner at the outset, so you can probably cut me some slack. What I am trying to demonstrate is that the lie that we are "captains of our souls" has a poetic resonance to those souls precisely because they wish to usurp God as sovereign king.

In other words, mankind's fall and our subsequent sin is not simply a matter of bad behavior—it is nothing short of cosmic treason. As Dietrich Bonhoeffer wrote:

The Fall of man in God's creation is both inconceivable and unalterably inexcusable, and therefore the word "disobedience" does not exhaust the facts of the case. It is revolt. . . . It is defection.[6]

"Your life is what you make it" is the battle cry of the insurrectionist. It is treasonous. And it leads to death.

THE INVINCIBILITY OF MEEKNESS

This does not mean, however, that there is no empowerment for mankind, only that it does not come about through self-exaltation. It does not come from believing the lie that God is holding out on us, that the life we ought to have can be made only by ourselves.

The false gospels of self-actualization, self-fulfillment, and self-assertion seek power where it either cannot be found or can only be found sinfully. In contrast, Jesus says, "Blessed are the meek, for they shall inherit the earth" (Matt. 5:5 ESV). Paul says, "I . . . appeal to you by the meekness and gentleness of Christ" (2 Cor. 10:1) and "we were gentle among you, as a nurse nurtures her own children" (1 Thess. 2:7).

What are they commending as a thoroughly Christlike disposition? Power under control, I suppose you could say. But more accurately, *weaponized weakness*. Meekness is human weakness owned, perhaps even "boasted" in—not as a means of self-pity, but as a means of self-denial. And in a world relentlessly preaching the satanic heresies of self-deification, self-denial is the vessel of Christ's conquering Spirit. Meekness is weakness weaponized against the spirit of the age and the spirit of the Antichrist, because it is a full-hearted embrace of the reality that Christ's strength, which is omnipotent, is made perfect in our weakness (2 Cor. 12:9).

Again, this is not passivity. It is not spinelessness. Christian meekness is a fearless humility resting in the spiritual security of Christ.

Meekness means not having to have the last word. Meekness means not feeling like every online scrum and outrage du jour needs your two cents, much less your forty-five-minute point-by-point podcast debunking. Meekness isn't afraid of losing face, being seen as weak, being misjudged or underestimated. Meekness is not concerned that you feel the weight of it—and thus you do.

Every now and again I read some male diatribe against the feminization of the church, explaining why men don't go to church services. This explains the rise of alternate, tribal church experiences like "biker church" or "cowboy church." These men cannot abide church experiences that do not center on their feelings and interests. They are not secure enough for that.

It turns out that the hypermasculine man is a lot more fragile than we thought.

He must feel really uncomfortable with the Sermon on the Mount. Because only namby-pamby pushovers walk second miles and give shirts to those who ask for coats. The alpha male could not make heads or tails of "blessed are the meek."

The devil, we should add, hates meekness. He himself is not meek, and he does not nurture meekness among his unwitting quarry. Passivity, yes. Meekness, no.

What the devil wants from Christians is aggressiveness and assertive self-interest. If the Great Commandment is to love God first and our neighbor second, the enemy would love if we'd all just look out for "number one." The feeding of our pride is a key campaign strategy for his minions, because "Pride comes before destruction, and an arrogant spirit before a fall" (Prov. 16:18).

In the end, those who believe they are in control of their own lives will discover themselves in a wasteland of their own devising.

But the meek? They will live forever.

YOU ARE ONLY OWED ONE THING

Several years ago a pastor I know offered me a position at his large church. Over the phone, he basically said to me, "Jared, what's your dream job?"

I'd never been asked that before. It never seemed feasible. Nobody really gets their dream job. Even if we enjoy what we do for a living, it's rare we'd consider our position our dream job. But I was being asked, so I answered. I described a few things I felt aligned with my gifts and experience. "Why?" I finally asked.

"Because I want you to come do that here."

I was a little startled. I began to consider the possibilities, how I'd be "graduating" from a small rural church of about 120 to an urban multicampus enterprise of thousands. I thought about some of the compromises I'd have to make, some of the convictions I'd have to stifle. To work in that environment, I would have to break a few promises to myself and explain a few changes in my published ministry philosophy to others. But none of that meant the offer didn't appeal.

I know I'm a strange person, but I began to picture being shown all the kingdoms of the world below my mountain perch and being told, "All this can be yours . . ."

Of course, my friend was not the devil! He simply resonated with my ministry, appreciated my gifts, and felt that I'd be a valuable asset to his team. I'm still appreciative of his offer, even though I declined with my thanks.

I have said yes to far more significant compromises over the years. I have never been glad I did.

I watch movies like *The Firm*, in which Tom Cruise's workaday lawyer is wined and dined by a high-powered outfit secretly in bed with the mob. He goes from ramshackle apartment and dinky car to gated mansion and luxury sedan. I think of another one of those Faustian derivations, *The Devil's Advocate*, where Al Pacino's devil similarly upgrades Keanu Reeve's country lawyer to New York penthouse riches.

I don't drive a fancy car or live in a mansion. Compared to most of the world's population, I am incredibly wealthy, but compared to many of my suburban compatriots, I am not living a life nearly indulgent enough. I don't really aspire to, but these scenes in these movies appeal to me. I like nice things. I think sometimes it'd be nice not to have to worry about figuring out how to pay for things like braces and unexpected medical bills and college tuition. I want to be wined and dined.

Your Faustian bargain may not be as extravagant. Maybe you just want to keep a little bit more of your income each year, so you figure the IRS won't notice if you fudge a bit here or there on your taxes. Or maybe your pact with the enemy has nothing to do with money at all. Maybe it's about the way you justify looking at porn each night. Maybe it's the way you rationalize taking unethical shortcuts at work. Maybe it's the gluttonous way you eat, with every day being a "cheat day," every unhealthy meal a prize you give to yourself for all you put up with.

It could be a big sin or a little sin, but all of it is a big deal. All of it is predicated on the idea that we are *owed*. Getting what we want is somehow just, we imagine, or at least closer to just than not getting it.

But there is only one thing we are owed—the judgment that we are desperately trying to avoid.

God says, "Don't eat this fruit. You will die."

The devil says, "Fake news. You deserve this."

We say, "I mean, surely a little bit won't hurt."

We all have sinned and fall short of God's glory (Rom. 3:23). We've all made the pact. Paul says in Ephesians 2:2 that we've all lived according to the devil.

Living as if life is what we make it is a lie from the pit of hell, which is what is owed to everyone who lives according to this lie. Damnation is the only thing we're owed.

And there's only one way out of paying what's due.

LIFE IS WHAT *HE* MAKES IT

"The wages of sin is death," Paul writes in Romans 6:23. This is the problem. It stands in stark relief to what we imagine the problem to be.

Go to the nearest bookstore in your town and find the self-help section. Chances are, it is one of the largest sections in the store, maybe even as expansive as the fiction offerings. Peruse the titles and subtitles. Make a mental tally of all the offers they make and lessons they promise. They will propose a variety of sources of our problems—personality, upbringing, family, diet, culture, work, fear, insecurity. The list could go on and on. The problems may be out there or "in here," but I'm willing to bet none of them actually highlights the single most dangerous problem every single human being who has ever lived will ever face—we are by nature sinners who deserve condemnation from the holy God we've disobeyed.

The problems the self-help books promise to address are multitudinous. The solution they all proffer is one. The solution is *you*.

You are the answer to your problems, the self-help industry claims. I mean, first *this particular* book or set of DVD lectures or mainline marketing scheme or weekend motivational seminar down at the Ramada is the solution. But all of those things just want to help *you* implement the improvement *you* are capable of to unlock the power of *you*.

"Your life is what you make it," says both the snake and the snake oil salesman.

They get the problem and the solution wrong. The problem is sin. (The problem is us.) And since this is true, it makes no sense to think the solution can be found within. It must be found without.

"The wages of sin is death, but the gift of God is eternal life in Christ Jesus our Lord" (Rom. 6:23). As it turns out, if the world will be sorted out, it must be something the Lord does.

Every year brings a fresh crop of self-help books. Every generation sees its own set of motivational speakers and prosperity preachers. Every culture develops its own visions of utopia. And still the problem never goes away. We only discover new ways to commit the same old sins.

We need to be rescued. We need to be remade.

After Adam and Eve fall, they are immediately conscious of their shame and vulnerability. "We'll fix it," they say to themselves. So they make coverings for themselves out of fig leaves.

When the Lord calls them to account, he lets them know that the death they've brought into the world cannot so easily be concealed. And yet he does not wish to leave them naked and afraid. Instead he covers them with the skins of animals.

This is perhaps the first instance of sacrificial covering, long before the official institution of the sacrifices in the Levitical system.

"You cannot cover you," the Lord says. "But I can. And I will."

To understand the depths of God's mercy, we must face honestly the depths of our depravity. We have indeed tried to live self-made lives in a self-made world. We have indeed made a mess of the whole place. Apart from grace, we traffic in death every godforsaken day.

> But God, who is rich in mercy, because of his great love that he had for us, made us alive with Christ even though we were dead in trespasses. You are saved by grace! (Eph. 2:4–5)

He has made this world, and he has made it good (Gen. 1:31). He's not going to let a bunch of sinners screw it up. No, the same God who has pronounced the curse in response to our sin has pronounced a blessing in response to the curse. He has sent his son to live the perfect life that Adam did not, to perfectly obey—and to perfectly sacrifice. Where Adam and Eve sought to "live forever" and so died, Jesus Christ so dies that we might live forever.

His resurrection, bodily and gloriously, is the first fruit (1 Cor. 15:20) of the resurrections still to come for those who trust in him. And one day he will return again, ushering in a new heavens and a new earth (Isa. 65:17; 2 Peter 3:13; Rev. 21:1) where his redeemed creatures may walk in peace with him for all of eternity future.

This world is what we've made of it. A cursed land where Satan roams freely. But the world we long for is the one the Lord is making through his Son and Spirit.

Hell will be full of self-made men.

There is only one thing left to do: deny yourself, take up your cross, and follow him (Luke 9:23).

YOU NEED TO LET GO AND LET GOD

This higher life as described is a will-o'-the-wisp,
an unreality that no one has ever laid hold of at all.

—J. I. PACKER, INTRODUCTION TO JOHN
OWEN'S *THE MORTIFICATION OF SIN*

YOU MAY NOT HAVE EVER HEARD OF THE KESWICK
theology, but you have likely heard some of its doctrinal claims
and hallmark slogans. You might have even repeated some of
them. Sometimes referred to as the "higher life movement," the
teachings held in prominence at the Keswick conventions of the
late nineteenth century have influenced countless evangelicals for
the past hundred years.

Keswick (pronounced *KEZ-ick*, silent *w*) is a place, not a person

THE GOSPEL ACCORDING TO SATAN

(though if it were, his first name would definitely be Alfred). A market town of Cumbria in England, Keswick became home to numerous meetings begun by an Anglican and a Quaker, influenced by various Wesleyan, Pentecostal, and revivalist-type strands in the church. Keswick theology promoted the potential for breakthrough in the Christian life: an instant experience of sanctification that would take serious believers to the next level in their discipleship.

Early Keswick conventions were organized around the process to this breakthrough, during which believers were said to confront a spiritual crisis, activate an experience of consecration, and then receive the Spirit's filling.

This may sound strange to you, but the influence of the Keswick movement has been far-reaching. Early proponents include authors of numerous classic devotionals, such as Andrew Murray and Hannah Whitall Smith, missionaries Amy Carmichael and Hudson Taylor, and pastors and denominational leaders such as D. L. Moody, R. A. Torrey, and the Christian and Missionary Alliance founder, A. B. Simpson.

If you've ever heard references to the "victorious Christian life" or to "letting go and letting God," you have heard Keswick ideas. In fact, the phrase "let go and let God," which we'll be considering in this chapter, comes directly from Keswick theology—and contains within it many of the problems of that perspective.

"Let go and let God" sounds good. It makes a certain kind of sense to spiritually minded people. I probably see this phrase, or some variation of it, in the comments on a friend's or family member's Facebook page weekly. Any time someone is struggling with a decision, agonizing through a crisis, or muddling through a season of doubt or confusion, some well-meaning religious person offers up, "Just let go and let God."

But what does that even mean?

On the surface, "let go and let God" is an exhortation to surrender one's will to the Lord. Taken charitably, it could be read as a call to repent of our own self-interested agendas and to trust in God. But we already have that kind of biblical language. So why don't we say "repent and believe" instead?

I think it's because we don't really mean "repent and believe." We say "let go and let God" to people struggling, hurting. It is seen as a solution to a problem out of our control.

"So what do I *do* to let go?" the recipient of this advice may ask.

"Well," replies the advice-giver, "you let go."

"Yes, but what does that look like?"

"It means stop trying to control things."

"But I'm already not controlling things."

"No, you're trying to control it by not letting go."

"So I'm not supposed to do anything?"

"No, the thing you do is let go."

If you're confused, it's because it's confusing. What the Keswick higher life theology teaches is a division between "Spirit-filled" Christians and "carnal" Christians. The Spirit-filled Christian accesses blessings in apparently automatic fashion, while the carnal Christian is still stuck "trying."

At its best, "let go and let God" is simply about repenting of anxious worrying and instead trusting God with our cares. This is something the Bible doesn't just permit, but commands. But without biblical thinking behind it, "let go and let God" can be a stumbling block for people who are suffering or in the midst of deep doubt or confusion, things for which spiritual clichés cannot help.

In this way, "let go and let God" as a means of experiencing the Spirit resembles the teaching we see in the "health and wealth" prosperity gospel movement. For one, it assumes being filled with the Spirit comes primarily through experiences of strength or achievement, rather than through weakness and suffering. The prosperity gospel has little truth to offer the poor or the chronically ill—except that they need to "have more faith."

"Let go and let God" promises a kind of formula of breakthroughs in exchange for faith; thus, if you're not experiencing the breakthroughs, it's because you don't have a strong faith or a big faith or any faith at all. You haven't "let go." The doctrinal snake eats its own tail, and it leaves believers confused, hurt, and spiritually decimated. You can never be enough or believe enough to achieve the ever-rising next level.

You may think this is much ado about nothing. The Keswick movement today, I am glad to say, has undergone a significant shift in its dominant theology and is now more aligned with traditional views of sanctification and more found in Reformational thinking. The late John Stott had a huge hand in this transition, and today theologically solid scholars and preachers such as D. A. Carson, Sinclair Ferguson, Liam Goligher, and Alistair Begg speak at the Keswick conventions.

But "let go and let God" persists. And while it sounds right, it will prove dangerous. No less a titan of doctrine than J. I. Packer was once endangered by higher life theology. Packer recalls his early wrestling within the Keswick school to "finally consecrate" himself to God and achieve the victorious Christian life:

Rather than meet temptation directly (which would be fighting in one's own strength), one should hand it over to Christ to deal with, and look to Him to banish it. Such was the consecration-and-faith technique as I understood it . . . the precious secret of what was called victorious living.

But what happened? I scraped my inside, figuratively speaking, to ensure that my consecration was complete, and laboured to "let go and let God" when temptation made its presence felt. At that time I did not know that Harry Ironside, sometime pastor of Moody Memorial Church, Chicago, once drove himself into a full-scale mental breakdown through trying to get into the higher life as I was trying to get into it; and I would not have dared to conclude, as I have concluded since, that this higher life as described is a will-o'-the-wisp, an unreality that no one has ever laid hold of at all, and that those who testify to their experience in these terms really, if unwittingly, distort what has happened to them. All I knew was that the expected experience was not coming. The technique was not working. Why not? Well, since the teaching declared that everything depends on consecration being total, the fault had to lie in me. So I must scrape my inside again to find whatever maggots of unconsecrated selfhood still lurked there. I became fairly frantic.[1]

And frantic is what most people who are told to "let go and let God" already are. Think of the pain this can cause the tender conscience, the already-weak believer feeling the weight of conviction. Chasing this spiritual phantom can be as exhausting as it is demoralizing.

Andy Naselli has written the best concise evaluation of

Keswick theology. Titled *No Quick Fix*, it is quite thorough and incisive despite its relative brevity. Naselli cut his ministry teeth in a church tradition devoted to higher life theology, and while he readily affirms the good in the teaching—a seriousness about holiness, an experiential and devotional approach to the Christian life—he is sober-minded about its deficiencies. According to Naselli, the thinking represented by "let go and let God" is chiefly beset by these ten problems:

1. DISJUNCTION. It creates two categories of Christians.
2. PERFECTIONISM. It portrays a shallow and incomplete view of sin in the Christian life.
3. QUIETISM. It emphasizes passivity, not activity.
4. PELAGIANISM.* It portrays the Christian's free will as autonomously starting and stopping sanctification.
5. MISREADING. It does not interpret and apply the Bible accurately.
6. FALSE ASSURANCE. It assures spurious "Christians" they are saved.
7. METHODOLOGY. It uses superficial formulas for instantaneous sanctification.
8. ADDICTION. It fosters dependency on experiences at special holiness meetings.
9. ABUSE. It frustrates and disillusions the have-nots.
10. SPIN. It misinterprets personal experiences.[2]

---

* *Pelagianism*, named for the fourth-century monk Pelagius, holds that human nature is untainted by sin and that the human will is free without any help from God to sin or not sin. The church declared Pelagianism heresy in the fifth century.

These are serious problems, to be sure, and several of them are especially bound up in the bad advice to "let go and let God." But the problem with this slogan isn't just that it's unclear. It's not just *squishy*. "Let go and let God" is spiritually dangerous and can lead to insecure Christians drawing conclusions our enemy would love for us to draw.

Why does the devil love "let go and let God"? Primarily because it is a superficial phrase ready-made to keep us chasing our tails and thus distracted from the deep things of God found in the press of affliction. But he also loves it for at least three other reasons, which we will examine one at a time. The three main problems with the advice to "let go and let God" are that:

1. It promises a super-Christianity that is impossible to attain.
2. It posits a doctrine of God that is weak and unbiblical.
3. It promotes a passivity in the Christian life that is essentially antinomian.

THERE IS NO CHRISTIANITY 2.0

Ten years ago I wrote a book called *Gospel Wakefulness*, which remains the single best outline of my entire ministry philosophy. It has been mostly well received, and I continue to speak on its themes today. *Gospel Wakefulness*—the book and the concept— was not without its critics, however. The experience I have labeled "gospel wakefulness" refers to the work of personal revival, the moment (or series of moments, usually) when a Christian becomes "awake" to the centrality of the finished work of Christ. For many of us, this marks the moment we realized that the good news of the free grace in Jesus was the grounds not only of our justification but also of our glorification—and the daily power of our sanctification every day in between. This has tremendous implications for how we view discipleship, holiness, and even preaching and teaching.

My friend Trevin Wax, who generously provided an endorsement for *Gospel Wakefulness*, was also not shy about sharing concerns about it.[3] Trevin's biggest concern is that it proposes a two-tiered Christianity, dividing people between "sleepy" and "wakened." The idea raises the specter of Keswick theology, which claims there are essentially three categories of people: unbelievers, carnal believers, and Spirit-filled believers. Trevin asked if the concept of gospel wakefulness was my version of a "second blessing" experience akin to that found in higher life thinking—or even a "Spirit baptism" experience like that encouraged in many Pentecostal and charismatic circles.

Like my friend Trevin, I am concerned about the alleged division of believers between carnal and spiritual. I remember firsthand the confusion and conflict stirred up by the so-called lordship salvation debate of the late seventies and early eighties. I have no desire to encourage any kind of varsity-level faith that might easily morph into a division between allegedly real Christians and false ones. Because that's typically how these kinds of categorizations go. And it is typically softhearted, convicted, genuine saints who feel the brunt of this division, fearing for the veracity of their *own* salvation.

One of the chief emphases of my book on gospel wakefulness is that the experience of personal revival results not in looking for some higher plain of spiritual existence but in staring at and drinking in the immeasurable riches of Christ that are totally available to every believer, wakened or not, because it is Christ who is big, not us. I wrote in the book:

> You are no less justified the moment of your salvation than you are ten minutes or ten years later, but the warp speed sanctification of gospel wakefulness may make you feel as though you were. What I'm trying to say is that Christ's sacrifice on the cross and resurrection out of the grave are big enough, grand enough, effective enough, and eternal enough to cover your shoddy Christian life, assuming of course you do believe.
>
> This is in fact the thrust of the gospel: it is Christ's work that saves, not yours. Be careful, then, not to attribute your continuing sinfulness or moments of depression to a lack of salvation. For one thing, people who are not truly saved generally don't worry about whether they are or aren't anyway—your anxiety on that matter is evidence of a reborn heart. But for another thing, this will only set you up for more trouble later on, because gospel-wakened people don't stop sinning either. If the measure of your perfection is the measure of your assurance, you will always be a timid, fearful Christian.[4]

"Let go and let God" as a problem-solver is a way of suggesting that faith is a force field against trouble. When we say "let go and let God" to those who struggle, we must be careful we aren't suggesting to them that if they were stronger Christians they wouldn't deal with such things. "Let go and let God" can inadvertently promote the idea that there are Christians, and then there are *Christians*.

There is no Christianity 2.0. Every believer in Jesus—whether new or old, immature or experienced, weak or strong—has received every spiritual blessing in Christ (Eph. 1:3). Every believer is totally and inextricably united to Christ for all eternity. There is no partway in. Every Christian is justified totally, freely, forever. In this regard, no one is higher or more advanced than any other. Christianity is not Scientology. It's not a pyramid scheme.

Like those within the lordship controversy who (wrongly) argued that one could receive Christ as Savior but not as Lord, "victorious Christian life" kinds of Christians don't just distinguish justification from sanctification but, in a sense, make them entirely dichotomous, as if you can have the former without the latter. Here's Andy Naselli again:

> Higher life theology chronologically separates justification from progressive sanctification by emphasizing a crisis of consecration that occurs at a point in time *after* justification and enables progressive sanctification to begin. That essentially divides Christ as one whom people can "take" as their justifier (or Savior) without "taking" him as their sanctifier (or Lord).
>
> But the New Testament teaches that from the moment of justification, progressive sanctification is experientially actual (not merely potential or possible) for all Christians. It is impossible for a Christian to be justified without at the same time experiencing progressive sanctification. That theme features prominently in Romans 5–8.[5]

Now, why would the devil give two bits about this weird theological debate? Is it because he likes when Christians argue about theology? Well, only if the wrong side appears to be winning the day. But the reason the devil is interested in this debate, and why I am convinced he is likely to stoke it in the hearts of many churches, is because it creates division. Further, it creates division between God's people by feeding the pride of one side and the insecurity of the other.

If Satan cannot keep you from salvation, he will do his best to undermine and obscure the gospel that saved you by making you either overconfident in yourself or underconfident in God. Both dispositions make the gospel look small and consequently may prevent more people from believing.

"Let go and let God" as advice to struggling people imagines there is some next-level Christian experience just waiting for us to crack the faith code. Like Luke Skywalker staring at the swamp trying to use his feelings to raise the X-Wing, we aren't quite sure how to accomplish something so big by doing so little. Do we think about it hard? Or not at all? Do we concentrate? Or do we empty our mind?

Our enemy would love to get us off the comfort we could have in knowing that no matter what our difficulties, we are already close to God through union with his Son by faith, and he would love to get us on the insecurity that comes from constantly worrying if our faith is strong enough. The best way to rattle your assurance is to keep measuring it. And the best way to undermine your confidence in your justification is to begin holding your sanctification up to the imaginary light of the Super Christian.

It doesn't take long for those who've been trying to "let go and let God" to let go of the process entirely, finding it futile and anxiety-inducing. "Let go and let God" is a lie that will ironically make you feel farther from God, not closer.

But there's another reason the devil is fond of this fortune-cookie faith, and it has to do with the view of God it promotes.

YOU DON'T "LET" GOD DO ANYTHING

An early proponent of Keswick theology once wrote, "Christians need not sin, and if they allow the Holy Spirit to 'operate invariably' they will not sin."[6] There are numerous problems in this one sentence, not least of which is that it represents, again, a fundamental misunderstanding about how sanctification works in a Christian's life. Another issue is the idea that Christians can reach a point of sinlessness (or near-sinlessness). But a big problem hiding behind the others is one that is repeated in countless Christian sermons, books, social media thoughts, and even songs. It is the notion of "letting God."

We must "allow the Holy Spirit" to operate, W. H. Thomas says.

I don't know if you noticed, but this sounds a lot like the Holy Spirit is our servant, a cosmic butler of sorts, rather than—oh, I don't know—the third Person of the Trinity and thus our *God*.

I get the heebie-jeebies when I come across language like this, which is a lot more often than I would like. Christians who ought to know better routinely begin statements with phrases like "God can't . . ." or "God needs . . ." We are told that we need to "let God" do all manner of things before he can guide us, bless us, reward us, and so on.

To all of this we ought to say that any God who needs us to activate him is not much of a god at all.

God says, "Look, I am the Lord, the God over every creature. Is anything too difficult for me?" (Jer. 32:27). He doesn't need our help. And he doesn't need our permission.[7]

One reason the serpent wished Adam and Eve to elevate their conceptions of themselves to godlike status is because he wishes by implication to demote the one true God to man-like status.

Satan loves "let God" language because he loves the idea of a deficient God. He will support any doctrine of God that is weak and unbiblical.

The true God is sovereign over all. If he does not do something, it is because ultimately he has willed not to do it. The blessings we receive in response to our honoring God are themselves foreordained. Even the faith we exercise to receive his salvation, which was until then withheld, is itself a gift from him (Eph. 2:8). And contrary to higher life teaching, the power we need to pursue holiness, choose obedience, and participate in our sanctification is granted entirely by God's grace.

"I labor for this," Paul writes in Colossians 1:29, "striving with *his strength* that works powerfully in me" (emphasis added). And when he tells us in Philippians 2:12 to "work out your own salvation with fear and trembling," he adds, "For it is *God* who is working in you both to will and to work according to his good purpose" (2:13, emphasis added).

Still, the language of "letting God" persists. A simple Google search of incomplete phrases like "you have to let God" and "God can't bless you unless . . ." returns an abundance of distressing results, including from high-profile evangelical leaders and otherwise reliable Christian resources.

It sounds true. But why? It sounds true because we have smuggled a cause-and-effect kind of spirituality into our Christian thinking, which is more akin to the idea of karma and grossly misunderstands that God declares the end from the beginning and does whatever he pleases (Isa. 46:10).

The gospel according to Satan seeks to dethrone the true Sovereign and enthrone the subjects. And the full counsel of the true gospel is the right antidote to "let go and let God" thinking, because only the gospel reminds us that God is sovereign over us and our circumstances—including our good works (Eph. 2:10)—while at the same time empowering us for these good works.

Which leads us to the third major problem with "let go and let God."

THE GOSPEL IS NOT OPPOSED TO EFFORT, BUT TO EARNING

The quietist notion of "letting go and letting God" promotes a passivity in the Christian life that is essentially antinomian.[*] The clichéd idea of "letting go" leads Christians to forego their role in active, ongoing obedience to the law of God. Indeed, higher life thinking, while ostensibly concerned with serious, noncarnal Christianity, nonetheless nurtures a fleshly Christianity in encouraging passivity in its aspiration to holiness.

This is indeed a strange brew. Keswick theology has its origins in Wesleyan and other forms of perfectionism. One would think the emphasis on holiness and the victorious Christian life would create legalism. But in positioning the fulcrum to law-keeping as "doing less," "letting go," or—as many higher life teachers are prone to say—"trusting rather than trying," the operating system of Keswick theology is functionally antinomian.

Antinomianism's official form is not taught much in the church today, but we see its shadows over Christian thought,

---

[*] *Antinomian* is just the theology nerd's fancy way of saying it is "against" (anti-) "God's law" (nomos). The church declared antinomianism a heresy.

including within some popular evangelical circles. Most recently antinomianism has become the dominant background theology in the so-called hyper-grace movement occupied by some radical Lutherans and neo-Reformed types. Many of these folks are fond of saying that true antinomians do not exist, that antinomianism is simply a boogeyman created by de facto legalists (of course) who are afraid of the full embrace of the Reformational hallmark *sola gratia* ("grace alone"). But of course they would say this. Antinomianism is usually expressed in a kind of doctrinal sleight of hand.

You can see the shades of this thinking whenever someone suggests that the commands of Scripture are not so much commands as they are "invitations." Author Tullian Tchividjian is an example of someone who positions imperatives (things we are told to do) this way. It makes for muddled biblical reading, as if Jesus and the apostles are incapable of saying what they mean. When Jesus says to "Go and sin no more" or "Go and do likewise," we are told that he doesn't really mean for us to obey, but rather to see that we cannot obey. It's as if every command in Scripture is an inverted Jedi mind trick or spiritual version of reverse psychology.

This is antinomianism because it abandons the so-called third use of the law. Traditionally, Reformed Christianity has held that the biblical commands serve three functions or uses:

1. A CURB. The law restrains sin as a model and guide for both Christians and non-Christians. We can see how the law serves as a deterrent in its application to the laws of nations and municipalities.

2. A MIRROR. The law reflects back our own unrighteousness as we see ourselves in its reflection. It is a standard

that, held against us, illuminates the reality of our depravity and our inability to perfectly obey.

3. A GUIDE. The law serves as our instructions, reliable commands that every person is obligated to obey.

The antinomian affirms the second use of the law but effectively ignores the third. Thus every command becomes merely a reminder of our inability to perfectly obey and, by insinuation, an impetus not to bother trying.

The antinomian argument is that grace is then championed. But in reality grace is cheapened, since it is not imagined that grace might both empower our sincere obedience and secure our faithful souls from equating our obedience with the salvation we are "working out." But as Dallas Willard has reminded us, "Grace is not opposed to *effort*, but is opposed to *earning*."[8]

The truth is that grace can be trusted to go all the way. We can obey God (by grace) and pursue holiness (by grace) as an implication of the justification (by grace) we have already received.

"Letting go and letting God," despite its alleged concern for avoiding carnality, functions as an essentially antinomian view of Christian spirituality because it encourages passivity in the pursuit of holiness. In direct response to the idea that we need to just "let go and let God," the late, great R. C. Sproul said:

We're to be actively engaged, not quietly waiting for God to do it for us, but at the same time not depending on our own powers and our own resources but realizing that this is a synergistic operation—a cooperative enterprise. I'm working. God is working. And He works through means. Those means of grace that He has given to us to help us in our sanctification: prayer,

Bible study, worship, fellowship, witnessing, and service. Those are the ordinary means of grace. You know, we're lazy, and we want sanctification in three easy steps. But, no. The whole process of sanctification is a lifelong enterprise of diligence and of commitment, making use of those means that the Lord has given to us. So, it's the lazy man's Christianity who says I'm going to sit back and let God do it for me.[9]

This is yet another reason why "let go and let God" is the gospel according to Satan: it truncates the gospel that the devil hates and violates clear commands to obedience, which the devil also hates.

If anyone tells you that you need to "just let go and let God," beware that you are receiving spiritually deformed spirituality. It is a religious sentimentality that may be coming from the forked tongue of the devil himself. "Let go and let God" makes a claim at selflessness—at getting ourselves out of the way—but it actually gets us focused on ourselves and our performance rather than on the powerful cross and the sufficiency of Christ's finished work. Christ's work is where, in order to spite this devil to hell, we will focus our attention in our final chapters.

THE CROSS IS NOT ABOUT WRATH

A God without wrath brought man without sin
into a kingdom without judgment through the
ministrations of a Christ without a cross.
—H. RICHARD NIEBUHR, *THE KINGDOM OF GOD IN AMERICA*

THE IDEA FOR THIS BOOK CAME FROM ANOTHER book I found by happenstance. One day I was perusing the religion section at Barnes & Noble and there, within the literary mélange of orthodoxy, heresy, and inspirational moralism, one title caught my eye.

Lies We Believe About God is by William Paul Young, author of the mega-bestselling novel *The Shack*. Intrigued, I withdrew it from the shelf and cracked it open. I hadn't even known that Young published nonfiction. I confess I could not get through even two chapters of *The Shack*, so I never got to all the parts where Young supposedly reinvents the Trinity and whatever. I just didn't enjoy the writing. But this book looked short and pithy, and it addressed a real need in the world: correcting misunderstandings about God.

As I looked over the book's table of contents, however, I began to see why all the charges of heterodoxy lodged at Young for *The Shack* might not have been overreactions. The chapter subjects, each allegedly a lie about God, included things that, depending on how you look at them, could be obvious misconceptions—things such as "God is a magician" or "Death is more powerful than God." But other subjects Young lists as lies most definitely are not. Here is a sampling:

- God is in control.
- God does not submit.
- God wants to be a priority.
- You need to get saved.[1]

To be clear, these are word-for-word statements from Young's book that he classifies as lies. And yet every single one of these things is a valuable truth that every person should know.

As I flipped through the book to peruse some of his rationales for categorizing true statements as lies, I was not helped much by the context found in the chapters. Each is very short, so there's not a lot of room for nuance, but what is bluntly there is plainly bad.

I thought to myself, *If the devil wrote a book about God, it might read just like this.* And, voila—the idea for *The Gospel According to Satan* was born.

I have chosen not to write this book from the perspective of

Satan for a couple of reasons. One, it's been done, and I am not C. S. Lewis. Two, I didn't relish the idea of trying to put myself in the devil's headspace, trying to think for an entire book in an inverted way about biblical ideas. It felt exhausting just to think about, and I assumed the experience would end up probably more than a little bit depressing spiritually.

But I wanted to plainly expose the claims and arguments that even many Christians make today that sound true and yet aren't. It is vital for every follower of Jesus to apply *what God really said* to every claim about what Jesus really said. It's one reason why I have included so many Scripture references. Publishing experts will often say these are distracting and turn off casual readers. That's all well and good, but this subject matter is not the kind of thing to take casually. The devil's lies are worth being alert about. So I have included as many Bible verses as I can to "show my work" so you can see where I'm getting my claims about God and his good news and determine whether I'm representing fairly what God says in his Word.

Young does not quote Scripture much. There is a sprinkling of Bible verses here and there, but he largely writes in platitudes and plausible arguments. The succession of chapters that most startled me in *Lies We Believe About God* were the ones about the atonement—that is, what Jesus accomplished spiritually in his death.

- Hell is separation from God.
- Sin separates us from God.
- The cross was God's idea.

These are all lies, according to Young. For good measure, he includes a further chapter titled "God Requires Child Sacrifice," a bald-faced attempt at stacking the deck against the idea of Jesus satisfying the wrath of God on the cross.

Using the title "God Requires Child Sacrifice" in a chapter arguing that the penal substitutionary atonement view (PSA) is a lie is a bit like the old gotcha: "When did you stop beating your wife?" *Of course* God doesn't demand child sacrifice. Of course that's not true. But neither is the idea that penal substitution is child sacrifice! Young wrote:

> How would we religious people interpret this sacrifice? We would declare that it was God who killed Jesus, slaughtering Him as a necessary appeasement for His bloodthirsty need for justice.[2]

And then:

> One of the narratives about God is that because of sin, God required child sacrifice to appease a sense of righteous indignation and the fury of holiness—Jesus being the ultimate child sacrifice.[3]

This is the caricature of PSA that Young clumsily props up so that he might clumsily knock it down. Referring to a blood-thirsty god who needs to have his sense of righteous indignation appeased, Young wants readers to think he is distinguishing a merciful, gracious God from a pagan conception of a capricious deity. Instead, he diminishes the holiness of God, downplays the seriousness of sin, and dismisses biblical language about God's ways with men.

Who else does that sound like?

IN RESPONSE TO THE HORROR OF THE CROSS

I don't mean to single out William Paul Young as an easy target. I should probably thank him for inspiring this book! But he represents a growing unease in evangelicalism with the concepts of a wrathful God and a propitiating* cross. More and more believers are listening to authors and pastors, mainly in the progressive or even postevangelical Christian tribes, who deny PSA and, like Young, refer to it with the worst language imaginable, saying something like, "To believe in PSA is to be a worshiper of a bloodthirsty god who violates his own laws against child sacrifice in order to commit cosmic abuse and murder against his own son."

Well, is that all?

Over the last several years, I have noticed this view gaining more ground in the evangelical marketplace and even among several circles of ministers I once considered likeminded friends. Denying PSA has become common among younger left-leaning Christians, the oft-called progressive evangelicals who listen to voices like Brian Zahnd, Pete Enns, or Richard Rohr.

A couple of years ago, after I had spoken on the cross at a Christian college, a young man approached me to inquire about my views of God's wrath and Christ's sacrifice.[4] I had not delivered a lecture on penal substitution or an extended excursus on the ins and outs of the doctrine of propitiation. I had merely articulated

---

* The concept of *propitiation* refers generally to "a payment that makes the receiver favorable." In relation to the biblical view of Christ's crucifixion, propitiation refers to the concept of Christ's death on the cross satisfying the wrath of God owed to sinners. Jesus has taken our place—*substituted* himself— and thus received upon himself the *penalty* for our sin. Thus, the "penal substitution" view of the atonement refers to Christ's taking the punishment for our sin so that God would look favorably toward us.

the good news that Jesus had taken the punishment for sin on the cross so that God's disposition toward those who believe in him would be not condemnation but everlasting life. Until then it had not occurred to me that this message would be controversial *among professing Christians.*

My new friend expressed distaste for the idea of a wrathful God. He used words like "bloodthirsty" and "child abuse." He didn't just prefer to prioritize other facets of the atonement; he repudiated penal substitution.

This is an important point to consider, because nearly all adherents to PSA whom I'm aware of do not deny that there are other facets of Christ's atoning work. These include views like the following:

1. CHRISTUS VICTOR: Christ's atoning work on the cross was about destroying the powers of evil, sin, and death, overthrowing Satan and his schemes and conquering death.
2. RANSOM: Christ's atoning work pays what is owed for rescuing human souls from bondage (depending on the view, from bondage to Satan, sin, or the Father).
3. MORAL EXEMPLAR: Christ's atoning work serves as an example of selfless sacrifice, undoing the self-interest of sin and providing a model for sinners in living godly lives.

It is true that some adherents to penal substitution appear unaware of these other facets of the atonement and seem to collapse them into PSA, wittingly or unwittingly. But few believe that PSA is the whole of Christ's atoning work. In my book *Gospel Deeps*, I dedicate a chapter to PSA, not meaning to equate it with the whole of Christ's atonement but as a way of arguing that PSA should be the "sharp point" first principle in our thinking.[5] I and most other Reformed adherents favor a multifaceted, synchronous view of Christ's cross.

The college student critiquing my gospel presentation may have favored such an approach, too, but for him there was no room in the cruciform symphony for the "penal" part of penal substitution. "Christ was our substitute, sure," many PSA-deniers say. "But he did not receive the wrath of God."

My response is typically, "Then who does?"

Who (or what) *does* take away the wrath God rightly owes sinners?

In the pursuit of a view of the atonement that is less bloody, less dark, less offensive, we may be stumbling upon one that is less effectual, less powerful, less . . . well, *atoning*.

The devil loves this development, because if he can get us to stop thinking about God's wrath at the cross, he can get us to stop thinking about how our sin is an offense to God, which means he can get us distracted from God's holiness and, thus, our need for salvation. The cross is not *only* about wrath, of course, but if we lose this vital aspect of Christ's atoning work—that he made propitiation by his death for sinners, that he was sacrificed as the penalty for our disobedience—we lose the very heart of the good news.

Still, the objections remain.

Does PSA depict a God who commits divine child abuse? The answer is an emphatic no. Abuse is committed with malice against unwilling parties. There is much to unpack theologically within this objection to PSA, including trains of thought that run through the stations of divine sovereignty, the divine operations within the triune Godhead, divine impassibility (the doctrine that

God does not experience pain or pleasure from the actions of another), and even divine eternality and the nature of time. But we look at the biblical witness to discern the portraits of the Father and the Son that God himself wants us to see in relation to the crucifixion of Jesus. And while the motif of the Son as a sacrifice is obviously there, we nowhere get a picture of a short-tempered God venting or taking advantage of his son.

On this subject of PSA making Christ the victim of divine abuse, the authors of *Pierced for Our Transgressions* wrote:

> First, according to the doctrine of penal substitution, Jesus willingly went to his death, in the full knowledge of what would be entailed. This is abundantly clear in the Gospels. For example, when Peter tried to deter Jesus from taking the path of suffering and death, Jesus denounced him with the words "Get behind me, Satan!" (Mark 8:33). Moreover, Jesus explicitly insisted that nothing compelled him to suffer and die against his will: "I lay down my life—only to take it up again. No-one takes it from me, but I lay it down of my own accord" (John 10:17–18). By contrast, child abuse involves inflicting pain upon an unwilling victim, or exploiting a person who is unable to understand fully what is happening.[6]

God's wrath is not abuse, because God is neither capricious nor short-tempered, because Christ goes to the cross willingly and consciously, because the cross was the triune God's idea from the foundation of the world, and because sin actually deserves punishment. For God to pour his wrath onto the Son at the cross is to uphold the justice reflective of their perfect righteousness. In fact, to think of God's wrath for sin as a short-fused reaction to irritations is like saying, "Gee, God, sin isn't *that* serious," which is like saying, "Gee, God, you're not *that* holy."

Derek Rishmawy has composed one of the best summations available online of answers to common objections to PSA, including moral, theological, and historical defenses. As much of William Paul Young's concern revolves around the alleged evil of retributive justice, it is worth quoting from Rishmawy's "The Beauty of the Cross: 19 Objections and Answers on Penal Substitutionary Atonement" here:

> Retribution can be part of a broadly restorative aim. Christ's penal death was not simply a strict act of retributive justice whose sole aim was to satisfy God's wrath or a strict, economic *tit for tat* exchange of punishment for sin. God could have had that by simply leaving people in their sins so that they might pay out their just wages, death (Rom. 6:23a). Instead, God's atoning act through the cross transcends strict retributive exchange, not by ignoring, but by fulfilling the claims of justice and pushing past them to the gift of God which is eternal life in Christ Jesus (Rom. 6:23b). God did not simply want to deal with sin; he wanted to save sinners. God did not only want to be vindicated as just, but instead wanted to be both "just *and* the justifier of one who has faith in Jesus" (Rom. 3:26).[7]

What objectors to PSA are running up against is the abject horror of the cross. And there should be no prettying up of this matter from any side of the atonement debate. The cross is a horrific thing. Jesus Christ really did die an anguished, mangled, torturous, bloody death on a Roman cross at the place called the

Skull. We're under no obligation to tidy it up and make it fit aspirational notions of human uplift and religious progress. If you skim quickly through the Old Testament and stop at the Gospels, you will see that Golgotha sits there at the end of a long, long conveyor belt of propitiatory slaughter.

Here is theologian Timothy George on what is occurring, and what is at stake, in the move to reject PSA:

> The problem comes when we use an anthropopathic term like "wrath" and apply it univocally to the God of eternity. Before long, we have constructed "a god who looks like me," to use the title of a recent book of feminist theology. Then caricatures of divine wrath proliferate: God having a temper tantrum or acting like a big bully who needs to be "appeased" before he can forgive or, as is often alleged with reference to the atonement, practicing cosmic child abuse.
>
> But God's ways are not our ways, and God's wrath is not like our wrath. . . . [Tony Lane writes,] "Without his wrath God simply does not love in the sense that the Bible portrays his love." God's love is not sentimental; it is holy. It is tender, but not squishy. It involves not only compassion, kindness, and mercy beyond measure (what the New Testament calls grace) but also indignation against injustice and unremitting opposition to all that is evil.[8]

The cross is an offense, a scandal (1 Cor. 1:18; Gal. 5:11). We should beware any view of the cross that seeks to make it more palatable to "more enlightened" sensibilities. We should be on guard against any theory of the atonement that promises fulfillment, beauty, and enlightenment apart from the blood of Jesus.

PROPITIATION IS NOT AN INNOVATION

Yet another objection to PSA is the idea that it is historically recent, that it is not found in the teachings among the fathers of the early church. Critics note the serious development of the view during the Reformation period of the sixteenth and seventeenth centuries and argue that it is not found before that.

Of course, every significant theological view supported by the Bible has seen its time frame for doctrinal development in the history of the church, dependent largely on cultural factors and the polemical needs of the day. We can chart how the church spent considerable efforts at distinct times formulating its doctrines of the incarnation, the Trinity, and the like. These were usually precipitated by major challenges within the church, the rise of heresies, or other crises. For the Reformers, exploring the facets of the atonement was largely driven by the greater issue of justification at stake in the Roman Catholic tradition. But is it true that PSA was not found in the early church at all? Did the Reformers, as some charge, invent it?

Not quite. That a view is not substantively and deeply developed until a certain era in church history does not mean it was not affirmed or articulated in previous eras.

Theologian Michael Vlach has done an admirable job chronicling the appearances of penal substitution in the writings of the fathers,[9] citing Clement of Rome, Ignatius, the Epistle of Barnabas, the Epistle to Diognetus, Justin Martyr, Eusebius of Caesarea, Eusebius of Emesa, Hilary of Poitiers, Athanasius, Basil the Great, Gregory of Nazianzus, Ambrose of Milan, John Chrysostom, Cyril of Alexandria, Gregory the Great, Severus of Antioch, Oecumenius, and of course Augustine of Hippo. Vlach's significant documentation spans the first ten centuries of the orthodox church.

In the end, however, the most important matter in this discussion is not what is said or not said by certain figures in church history, but *what does the Bible say?*

Is penal substitution a biblical idea?

The first thing we need to examine is whether God's wrath is ever said in the Bible to be directed toward *people*—or is it only aimed at sin or the devil and his demons? And you don't have to look very deeply to see the answer is yes, it is often aimed (or said to be "owed") to people.

In Exodus 15, for instance, the celebratory song of Moses about the freedom of the Israelites from Egyptian bondage includes mention of God's "burning wrath" against his enemies (v. 7).

Second Chronicles 36:16 reads, "But they kept ridiculing God's messengers, despising his words, and scoffing at his prophets, until the LORD's wrath was so stirred up against his people that there was no remedy."

Consider Psalm 90:11: "Who understands the power of your anger? Your wrath matches the fear that is due you."

We could go on and on. These are just three examples from nearly two hundred entries that feature the word "wrath." We could search for examples of God's "anger" or "vengeance" or "justice," and we would add far more to the tally. The point is that the Bible's teaching on God's wrath is not unclear. It is real, it is justified, and it is owed to those who disobey him. In Ephesians 2:3 Paul writes that unsaved persons are "by nature children under wrath."

Next we must look and see what God has established in his relations with people to "turn away" that wrath. How is it that we might avoid God's wrath and experience not his condemnation but his salvation? The Bible shows that this begins and ends with the blood of sacrifice.

From the covering of Adam and Eve with animal skins to the long-standing institution of the sacrificial system, the motif of propitiating blood is everywhere one turns in the Old Testament. The Passover is perhaps the most notable illustration of this dynamic, in which the children of Israel must paint the blood of a lamb across their doorposts to avoid the Lord's striking their firstborn dead. Any house marked with this blood was "passed over." Any house that was not, received the due penalty.

It is the God-instituted Passover, in which a spotless lamb is killed and its blood used to mark the forgiven, that centers the sacrifices thereafter, which culminate in the sacrifice of Christ himself, who is called the Lamb of God.

Of course, the most notable Old Testament passage on penal substitution is found in Isaiah 53:5–6:

> But he was pierced because of our rebellion,
> crushed because of our iniquities;
> punishment for our peace was on him,
> and we are healed by his wounds.
> We all went astray like sheep;
> we all have turned to our own way;
> and the LORD has punished him
> for the iniquity of us all.

This passage clearly teaches that the suffering servant, whom we know this side of the Testaments is Jesus the Christ, was punished in our place and, moreover, that he was punished in our place *by God himself.*

Oddly, William Paul Young mentioned Isaiah 53 in his chapter on the cross, though it is an odd paraphrase, perhaps his own:

> Although he bore our sin and suffered at our hands, yet we considered him punished and afflicted and stricken by God . . . and in Jesus, God encountered/embraced [*paga* in Hebrew] our twisted rebellion and brokenness.[10]

The first part of his paraphrase resembles the passage, but the second part, after the mysterious ellipsis, does not at all. Young is attempting to recast Isaiah 53 as our misunderstanding of the cross. In other words, we "considered" Jesus punished on our behalf, but we were wrong. Which of course is not at all what the plain reading of Isaiah 53 says.

The critic of penal substitution may argue that all of the Old Testament passages only make sense to us in the light of the New, and they would be correct. So we look also to the New Testament teaching on the cross, which, as I mentioned, is multifaceted and deep, and yet throughout returns one particular resounding refrain: Christ has taken our punishment.

Think of the way Paul speaks of the atonement merely throughout his letter to the Romans. In chapter 6, verse 23, he clearly says that what is due for our sin is death. The wage owed is death. In 1:32, he says that sinners "deserve to die" and that this is "God's just sentence." (This is perfectly in keeping with the wrath/judgment theme running throughout the Old Testament.) What's the way out of paying what we owe, then? In Romans 3:25, Paul wrote this:

> God presented him [Christ] as an atoning sacrifice in his blood, received through faith, to demonstrate his righteousness,

because in his restraint God passed over the sins previously committed.

Many translations include the word "propitiation" here in place of "atoning sacrifice," and while I acknowledge the tricky linguistics at work in the Greek text, the concept is clear as day to those who care to see it. Ditto 1 John 4:10: "God . . . sent his Son to be the atoning sacrifice for our sins."

In a book chapter dedicated to Romans 3, Mark Dever wrote:

> The point is that Christ's death removed the penalty of our
> sin by removing the wrath of God. Our sin is not the primary
> object of this sacrifice. It is not merely an expiation, or covering
> of sin, that takes place. No, the main point of Christ's sacrifice
> is not covering over our sins, though he does that, but rather
> the satisfaction of God's right wrath against us because of our
> sins. That's what the word *propitiation* indicates—the satisfac-
> tion of God's holy anger against us.[11]

In 1 Thessalonians 1:10, Paul writes that Jesus saves us "from the coming wrath." Jesus himself refers to "this cup" from the Father (Luke 22:42), and there is little serious doubt that this is a reference to the cup of God's wrath, a common covenantal symbol.

The curse motif is also an important thread in the cord of penal substitution. At the fall, God pronounced all creation under a curse. Notice that while we are consequently in bond-age to sin, endangered by the devil, vulnerable to hardships, and destined to decay, the ordination of the entire curse comes as part of God's judgment on sin. In other words we don't simply suffer the consequences of our bad decisions; we are deserving of punishment.

But Paul writes in Galatians 3:13 that Jesus became the curse for us. In effect, the Son willingly received what was owed to us—the wrath of God—that we might willingly receive what was owed to him—righteousness.

Nearly the entire book of Hebrews makes recurring connections between the propitiating and expiating sacrifices of the old covenant system and Christ's fulfillment of them on the cross.

The truth is that the Holy Spirit has inspired a painstaking case from Old to New Testament for Christ's propitiatory work on the cross. Therefore, the concept of propitiation is not a Reformation innovation. The church fathers affirmed it here and there, but the Bible itself teaches it everywhere.

Look, this is not some insignificant intramural debate. This is not just academic quibbling over theological minutiae. All of this matters, because what the Bible teaches us about salvation matters. It matters so much that if we get far off on the Bible's teaching about salvation, we bring into jeopardy our own salvation.

This is ultimately where I took it with the college student challenging my view of PSA. After walking him through the best biblical survey I could manage from memory and seeing he wasn't buying it, I just asked him directly, "Are you a sinner?"

He thought for a second, then said, "Yes."

So I asked him: "How is it that your sins are forgiven?"

He did not answer. I could tell he was mulling the question over.

I wondered if he'd never thought of it. I wondered if he had become infatuated enough with academic debates on the cross and the rejection of the blunt doctrine of his upbringing if he'd forgotten to take the cross not just intellectually or academically or theoretically, but *personally*.

I hope you are seeing what's at stake here. The problem with affirming *Christus victor* and the ransom motif or any other facet of the atonement to the exclusion of penal substitution is that we render impersonal what Christ did on the cross. He conquered the powers and the principalities and death itself. He achieved justice for the socially downtrodden and persecuted. He did anything and everything, all the wonderful and multitudinous things the Bible says he did, but he didn't do the one thing that would make me right with God. He didn't take my punishment.

In a short piece on "The Logic of Penal Substitution," J. I. Packer wrote:

> Gustaf Aulén characterized the Christus victor motif . . . as a dramatic idea of the atonement rather than a rationale of its mechanics, and contrasted it in this respect with the "Latin" view, of which penal substitution is one form; but should not penal substitution equally be understood as a dramatic idea, declaring the fact of the atonement kerygmatically, i.e., as gospel (good news), just as Aulén's conquest motif is concerned to do? I believe it should. Surely the primary issue with which penal substitution is concerned is neither the morality nor the rationality of God's ways, but the remission of my sins.[12]

And if we refuse to affirm Christ's taking of our punishment, we will have to take it ourselves. Either way, the wrath of God will be delivered for sin. He is too holy, too just, too righteous, and too perfect to "let it slide."

Let us be careful that our upending any other view of the

atonement over PSA is not an attempt to keep the cross at arm's length. Let us fear championing the impact of the cross on *those people* or *those issues* and not on us. Let us beware of not taking it personally.

The blood of the Lamb is too precious not to be applied to our own doorposts.

Packer again:

> To affirm penal substitution is to say that believers are in debt
> to Christ specifically for this, and that this is the mainspring
> of all their joy, peace, and praise both now and for eternity.[13]

This is why the claim that "the cross is not about wrath" is so devilish. It promises to help us avoid the sticky issue of wrath while actually keeping us in its crosshairs. Our enemy knows that if the wrath owed us is taken by Christ, we will experience joy, peace, and praise. We will get the fulfillment, beauty, and enlightenment we long for.

And he knows that if we try to get those things without the blood, we are agreeing to remain under the wrath that all disobedience deserves.

SATAN HATES THE BLOOD

The devil loves a bloodless cross. He doesn't mind a shiny trinket around your neck so long as it's not a shining treasure in your heart.

Satan is afraid of the blood. He knows it washes sinners clean (Heb. 9:14; 1 John 1:7; Rev. 7:14), that it speaks the word of justice accomplished (Heb. 12:24). He knows that the bloody cross spells his doom, that on the hill Golgotha, Christ "disarmed the rulers and authorities and disgraced them publicly; he triumphed over them in him" (Col. 2:15). And he knows the blood of Christ pays the wrath owed sinners (Rom. 3:23; 1 John 4:10), thereby forever making his accusations against God's people null and void.

The blood of Jesus spells the devil's doom. Which is why he would love for you to keep your gospel nice and respectable. Tidy. Academic.

In 1955, Billy Graham went to Cambridge to preach a series of sermons at the university.[14] Before his arrival, the English media had a field day in the papers expressing their disdain and skepticism about Graham's visit. According to Tim Keller, one editorial asked, "What in the world is this backwoods American fundamentalist doing coming to talk to our best and brightest?"

Graham was intimidated by the advance criticism. He was extremely nervous preparing his messages for the Cambridge crowd, comprised of university professors and doctors, theologians, and numerous other intellectual elites from the community. He mined books and papers for cultural and philosophical illustrations, adding quotes from Kierkegaard and Nietzsche and Sartre to his planned talks.

Graham was afraid of looking like a rube before the discriminating audience.

The first four nights, Graham bombed. The halls were packed but the response was tepid. His preaching did not elicit any significant response.

So on the last night, Graham decided to ditch the highbrow quotes and intellectual spice. He decided he was just going to preach on the blood. He decided that instead of trying to boast in his intellectual prowess, he was going to forget everything else and simply boast in the cross.

Anglican pastor and founder of the Proclamation Trust, Dick Lucas, later recounted:

> I'll never forget that night. I was in a totally packed chancel sitting on the floor with the Regius Professor of Divinity sitting on one leg, the chaplain of a college who was a future bishop on the other. Now, both of these were good men in many ways but they were completely against the idea that you needed salvation from sin by the blood of Christ. And that night dear Billy got up and started at Genesis and went right through the whole Bible and he talked about every single blood sacrifice you can imagine. The blood was just *flowing* all through Great St. Mary's everywhere for three-quarters of an hour. And both my neighbors were terribly embarrassed by this crude proclamation of the blood of Christ. It was everything they disliked and dreaded. But at the end of the sermon, to everybody's shock, about four hundred young men and women stayed to commit their lives to Christ.

Lucas later met a young curate and Cambridge grad at the Birmingham cathedral. Over tea he asked the man:

> "Where did Christian things begin for you?"
> "Oh," the curate said. "Cambridge, 1955."
> "When?"
> "Billy Graham."
> "What night?"

"The last night."

"How did it happen?"

He said, "All I remember as I walked out of Great
St. Mary's was for the first time in my life thinking,
Christ really died for *me*."

Tim Keller says that if you boast in anything other than the
cross, "the devil will outflank you." You must make it personal.
You must be able to say not merely that Christ died but that Christ
died *for me*.

GOD HELPS THOSE WHO HELP THEMSELVES

*The only thing we contribute to our salvation
is the sin that makes it necessary.*
—WILLIAM TEMPLE

MY FRIEND RAY LOOKED SERIOUS. HE ALWAYS LOOKED serious. But this particular day, over a breakfast of oatmeal and coffee in a Nashville hotel café, he looked more serious than normal.

I don't remember what we were talking about; I've lost the context of our conversation. But what he said at the end has stuck with me ever since. It was not something I hadn't heard before, but how Ray said it, and the extra seriousness with which he said it, latched into my mind and heart. It was probably about six years ago, and yet I have never forgotten it.

"Jared," he said. "The devil has a filing cabinet. And in that filing cabinet he has a file on you. He has a folder with your name on the tab. That folder contains exactly what it would take to make you fall."

I tried to hold his gaze, but the idea was startling.

"Satan knows exactly what will bring you down. And every day he is working that strategy to make it a reality."

As I said, I have not forgotten that conversation. I think about it often. I know it's true.

It's true for you too.

If you're not a believer in Christ, the first thing I would say is to not waste another second in unbelief. Jesus Christ lived the sinless life we could not, died the sacrificial death we would not, and rose again gloriously so that any sinner who trusts in him can be where they are not—and where he currently is. The time to repent of your sins and put your faith in him for forgiveness and eternal life is *now*.

The second thing I'd say is that whether you believe it or not, the devil is real. And if you don't trust in Jesus, you are exactly where the devil wants you.

If you are a Christian, I would say that our enemy is rabid for your destruction. He cannot kill your soul, for that is safeguarded with Jesus, but he would love nothing more than to lure you into sin, make a smoking crater of your life any way he can—as he did with Job—and render you ineffective for the kingdom and thus discredit the witness of the gospel. He wants to make Jesus look small in your life.

Here's what you and I have to do: we must, with the right kind of awareness of our accuser's strategies, consider what's written in his folder about us.

I've thought long and hard about what's in my file in hell's cabinet. Twenty years ago, I am fairly certain I would have said sexual immorality. I have never engaged in adultery with another woman, but there was a time when lust ruled my life. I believe I was a believer even then, but I was not walking in step with the truth of the gospel (Gal. 2:14). I had submerged myself in habitual porn use. It affected everything about me. Not just how I thought, but how I acted. In the end, I did make an utter wreck of my life.

I cannot say "the devil made me do it." That is a cop-out and a misunderstanding of the dynamic of temptation and disobedience. My sin was and is mine. I cannot blame it on anybody but myself. But the devil was working that file, and I was willfully falling into his trap.

I didn't know Ray twenty years ago, but if we were to have had our conversation at that time, I have little doubt that images of the end of the road of wanton lust would have flashed across my mind. Embarrassment. Shame. Adultery, perhaps. A wrecked marriage, certainly.

I am not a lust-free person today, by any stretch, but by the grace of God I live a daily life of conquest over that period in my life. I am, in those respects, "clean and sober." I know that if I think myself totally invulnerable to that old way of life, I should take double heed so that I don't fall again (1 Cor. 10:12).

But I think my folder today has a different strategy in it. What flashed across my mind when Ray issued that profound personal warning was not any gross physical sin or obvious behavioral infidelity, but rather a pattern of attitudes, thoughts, and insecurities that, when indulged, render me ineffective for the kingdom. In a way, this pattern is more dangerous than sexual sin, if only because it is harder to discern, harder to barricade myself against.

There is no accountability software or phone app to keep me from thinking about myself too much.

The devil doesn't care. He doesn't care if it takes my having an affair or my becoming an arrogant, prideful mess. He just wants to steal my hope, kill my worship, and destroy my witness.

In a lot of ways, this propensity for sinful insecurity goes all the way back to my childhood. It predates my infatuation with private lust. It has always rumbled in my heart, a storm in need of calming. It goes deeper than whatever behavioral manifestation it takes in any given season of my life. Sometimes it's off-putting sullenness. Sometimes it's abrasive arrogance. Sometimes it's divisive language. A lot of times it's just spiritual laziness and undisciplined blah.

I have an exceptionally difficult time distinguishing between the default melancholy of my personality and disobedience to commands to rejoice. I am, in short, a legalist. I am a legalist sometimes with others, but nearly all the time with myself.

My legalism doesn't always look pharisaical. I don't think I'm a religious nitpicker. I don't think I'm any more judgmental than anybody else who uses social media on a regular basis. Except I compare myself to those people a lot and polish my shirt collar. "I thank you, god of myself, that I'm not like *those* people."

The kind of legalism that seems part of my DNA is the kind that rots my bones and thus rots my sense of assurance. It *seems* humble, my kind of legalism, which is what makes it so insidious and, quite often, debilitating.

When I'm not priding myself on being more *whatever* than others, I hate myself for not being whatever *enough*. The weird thing about humility is that the more you think about it, the more it goes away. That's me. I dwell on both my accomplishments and my failures way too much. I stew. I worry.

Pride doesn't always look like arrogance. Sometimes it looks like self-pity.

I don't know how Satan has worded this in his file, but I think what it amounts to is that he knows I have an addiction to approval, to affirmation, and, consequently, to insecurity.

I want to be on guard against his temptations in these areas. Maybe you do too. That's why you and I both need to be very, very afraid of not just the proverbial *wording* of "God helps those who help themselves," but also the *spirit* of it. We rightly regard this saying as silly and cliché, but deep down way too many of us kind of believe it.

According to Barna research, 82 percent of Americans believe that "God helps those who help themselves" is a Bible verse.[1] You may suggest this only confirms the biblical illiteracy of our post-Christian nation. But it doesn't explain the reality that more than half of practicing Christians thought the same.[2]

It's not a Bible verse, by the way.

But maybe one of the reasons Christians project this onto the Bible—despite the idea originating in Grecian antiquity and hitting the proverbial wisdom of the mainstream through inclusion in Benjamin Franklin's *Poor Richard's Almanack*—is because it sounds true to our fleshly hearts.

When Adam and Eve fell from grace, humankind became wired for works.

WHY WORKS SALVATION IS SO TEMPTING

"God helps those who help themselves" is essentially a legalistic ethos. In many ways, it is the counterpoint to "let go and let God." Antinomianism and legalism are opposite (but equal) errors.

What this legalistic proverb literally suggests is that God does not help those who refuse to help themselves. It is related to "your life is what you make it." Like "let go and let God," it centers on self but in a much more pragmatic way.

But you should know that the very heart of true Christianity is opposed to the idea that God helps those who help themselves. The worldview this lie represents is antithetical to the grace that makes Christianity unique and saving.

Its nod to God is a subterfuge from Satan. He would prefer if we never thought of God at all, but the next best thing is to think wrong thoughts about him, thoughts that are not worthy of him.

If our enemy cannot get us off the subject of salvation entirely, he will get us onto it in the wrong ways—namely, by introducing even a small measure of works into the salvation equation. This lie has always been effective with religious people, for reasons that include a connection to the first lie covered in this book. Satan desperately wants us to add a "plus" to the gospel of grace, because that detracts from Christ and his sufficiency.

"God helps those who help themselves" sounds stupid to the theology of my head, but it sounds true to the wonky theology of my flesh. When I am down in the spiritual doldrums, I'm tempted to believe it. I am afraid that God doesn't, won't, can't love me. That my approval before him is based on my religious output, and of course, I am fully aware that I can never do enough.

Then I'm afraid that by thinking such unbiblical thoughts, I've really messed up, and I might not even be a Christian at all.

I told you I was a mess.

You would think grace would be so appealing. The very idea that despite our inability to measure up to God's glory, he freely and lovingly lavishes grace on us as a gift is refreshing and wonderful. We cannot get this message anywhere else. No other religion or philosophy offering fulfillment, beauty, and enlightenment teaches that those things are given unilaterally by the God of grace. How amazing is that?

And yet if this truth is really that appealing, more people would jump at the opportunity to believe it, wouldn't they? But we suspect it's not true. Even those of us who believe it's true struggle to live out that belief.

Our flesh yearns for works, for credit.

Paul's letter to the Galatians may be the best short treatment on the radical intrusion of grace into the God-dishonoring world of legalistic religion. The apostle is astounded that those who know about the free grace given in the good news of Jesus would abandon it. "Why in the world would you return to the slavery of works righteousness?" he wants to know (1:6; 5:1).

The Galatian church had become infiltrated by false teachers referred to as "Judaizers." They were arguing that Christianity is made up of grace *plus* works—in this case, the works of the Jewish ceremonial law, namely circumcision and the dietary restrictions. "Yes, yes, grace," the Judaizers said, "but also you need to be extra religious. That is how you earn approval with God and stay united to Jesus."

Through the plausible arguments of the Judaizers, the devil tempted many professing believers to make a shipwreck of their faith.

While Paul is astonished by the Galatians' preference for works righteousness over the free gift of Christ's righteousness, he knows that it is a tempting lure. He knows it "makes sense." And he knows it crouches at the door of every human heart, that no person is immune to its allure. In Galatians 6:15, Paul even warned the ones restoring those who've fallen prey to the heresy to watch out themselves, so they won't also be tempted into it.

It seems odd to think that if you were teaching grace to legalists, you'd be tempted to become a legalist yourself, but I am here to tell you it is a very real danger.

Once I was giving a guest lecture in a college classroom on gospel-centered ministry. During the Q&A, a student asked me one of the most profound and penetrating questions I've ever received in such an environment. He said, "I just want to know one thing: Do you preach the gospel to yourself as well as you do to us?"

I stopped for a second, weighing my options. My approval-meter kicked in, and I wanted to be seen as impressive. But I realized the truth might be more helpful to him—and to me. I replied, "No, I don't. I am much better at reminding others of grace than resting in it myself."

For one thing, we can become inordinately proud of being "grace people." And when we do that, we've instantly begun eroding our own credibility, perhaps not before others but certainly within our own hearts. For many Christian preachers and teachers, there is a real danger of giving grace to themselves while withholding it from others. All believers are in great danger of this disobedience to the Great Commandment. But for many there is also danger in preaching with our mouths what we don't believe in our hearts.

And yet there is grace even for that. Amazing. We find it in the true gospel of God saving those who cannot, despite their best intentions and efforts, help themselves.

Paul was upfront that the "God helps those who help themselves" mantra is not just another gospel (Gal. 1:6) but a satanic heresy (vv. 8–9). Referring to a similar kind of legalism in instructions to his ministry protégé Timothy, he called it demonic (1 Tim. 1:1–3).

Works righteousness is like that forbidden tree in the middle of the garden. We can see it in our midst. It is always within eyesight of our reveling in grace. And every now and again, we hear a serpentine whisper: "Yes, yes, grace. But there's more. There's an enhancement. There's real power, real enhancement *here*, with this. Take and eat."

And it's so tempting, because it promises to make much of us. Legalism pets our pride so smoothly.

"God helps those who help themselves" is the lie that promises to gratify our desire for recognition and reward. But in the end, it leads only to exile.

TO BE WORKING FOR SALVATION
IS TO ALWAYS BE WORKING

A couple of years ago, while speaking at a few events in Washington State, I found myself in an evangelistic conversation with an Uber driver named Nealofer. A devoted Muslim, Nealofer began the conversation trying to evangelize *me*. He started by asking if I was religious. I am never quite sure how to answer that question, because we all know that Christianity is "not a religion, but a relationship" (which isn't exactly true, but that cliché will have to wait for another book, maybe a sequel to this one if you buy enough copies).

Given the implied definition of "religious," I said that yes I was.

He asked what my religion was. I told him, and he commended me for following the prophet Jesus. (Muslims do not believe Jesus was actually God incarnate, only an important prophet who taught the truth.) He proceeded to tell me that the Bible was like first grade and the Koran was like fifth grade. "When you're done with first grade," he said, "you don't stay there, do you? You move on."

I suppose this is the Muslim's version of higher life theology.

I responded with a few questions of my own. I asked Nealofer if what we learn in first grade becomes untrue in fifth grade. For instance, if we learn our alphabet in first grade, do we read books using different letters in fifth? If we learned that 1+1=2 in first grade, does 1+1 stop equaling 2 in the fifth grade?

He said of course not.

"So," I said, "if we both agree that whatever the Bible said is true, then we have to agree that it's always true."

He agreed—that is, he agreed until I pointed to many places where the Bible directly affirms the deity of Jesus. I lost him there. So I went straight to the point:

"How do you get to Paradise?"

He said what nearly every person who believes in a heavenly kind of afterlife believes, only the Islamic variation of it, of course. You work. You obey. You become good enough.

I've had numerous conversations with Muslims like this— usually in cabs or Uber rides, actually—and I always ask the same follow-up:

"Do you think you're good enough?"

I asked this same question once of a cab driver in Minneapolis. He was honest enough to answer, "No."

Nealofer was much more confident in his righteousness. He said, "Yes."

"How do you know?"

"I just know," he said.

"Well," I replied, "you must be a better person than I am. Because I am not good enough."

Nealofer proceeded to argue with me about my goodness. He was sure I was a good person, very sure of it. I'm uncertain how he could gauge that from a fifteen-minute car ride. I mean, I said I was religious, I guess, and I didn't cuss or try to rob him even once, so maybe he thought he had a good read on me. But in any event, he talked me up. And I kinda liked it. But he was wrong. About him and about me.

I like Mormons. You probably do too. You'd have to be kind of a jerk not to. I voted for a Mormon (not the famous one) in the last presidential election—that's how much I like 'em. Mormons as a group have a well-earned reputation as exceptionally moral people, behaviorally speaking. And they know it. They have to be moral, because their doctrine of salvation depends on it.

A lot of Mormons want to be considered a part of the evangelical community today. It is a benefit to them, because it helps remove the stigma of their being a cult. It is a benefit to a lot of evangelicals, because we get more well-behaved people on the team.

But the blurring of doctrinal lines between Mormonism and orthodox Christianity is not a good thing. It's the kind of thing that Paul was all upset about in Galatians. Mormons' own sacred text says things such as, "Love God with all your might, mind and strength, then is his grace sufficient for you"[3] and "For we know that it is by grace that we are saved, after all we can do."[4]

Grace, *after* all we can do. That sounds a lot like "God helps those who help themselves," doesn't it?

If you want to know where the Mormon concept of grace comes from, ultimately, you only have to consider that they believe the Son of God is a created being who is spirit-siblings with Lucifer and that, as God himself was once a man, obedient Mormons can one day become a god like him. If this sounds familiar, it might be because we've looked at Genesis 3 several times already. The diminishing of God and the exaltation of man are satanic lies, and thus Mormonism is one of those doctrines of demons Paul warned about.

I ask the same question of my Mormon friends as I do my Muslim friends: How do you know you've done all you can do? How good is good enough?

The answer is that you can never know. "You just have to trust." But trust in what? Not the free grace of God, because remember, the grace-of-works religion is not grace at all but a reward for good behavior. So how good must I be to no longer fall short of the glory of God?

The answer is that we must be perfect.

Because of that, the pursuit of holiness as a means of salvation will be a never-ending pursuit with no arrival. We cannot work hard enough, climb high enough, or obey long enough to reach salvation by our efforts. To work for our salvation is to always be working, which means to work for our salvation is to never be saved.

"God helps those who help themselves" is a lie.

The devil wants us to believe this lie. But he is in trouble.

Every Christian who, unlike Eve, brings to mind "what God really said" has a filing cabinet too. And in that filing cabinet there is a folder with Satan's name on it. We know just what it will take to bring him down.

FIGHT THE DEVIL WITH THE RIGHT ARMOR

"Therefore," James the apostle says, "submit to God. Resist the devil, and he will flee from you" (4:7).

You want to take the devil down? You must actively resist him.

What does actively resisting him look like? It begins with what James says in the first part of that verse: submitting to God.

This entails daily pursuing repentance and engaging in the divine dialogue of hearing from God (through meditation on his Word) and talking to God (by prayer). There are other means of active resistance too—most notably, covenanting with a local Christian church and frequently singing songs of praise to God, both inside and outside of that church's gatherings—but the bottom line is that if we do not set our minds on God's glory and all the things he really said, we are making ourselves vulnerable to lies.

Trusting in our works makes us vulnerable to the enemy. It is like David donning the armor of Saul (1 Sam. 17:38–39)—we cannot walk in it.

Paul again helpfully tells us what to do to effectively resist the devil:

> Finally, be strengthened by the Lord and by his vast strength. Put on the full armor of God so that you can stand against the schemes of the devil. For our struggle is not against flesh and blood, but against the rulers, against the authorities, against the cosmic powers of this darkness, against evil, spiritual forces in the heavens. For this reason take up the full armor of God, so that you may be able to resist in the evil day, and having prepared everything, to take your stand. Stand, therefore, with truth like a belt around your waist, righteousness like

armor on your chest, and your feet sandaled with readiness for the gospel of peace. In every situation take up the shield of faith with which you can extinguish all the flaming arrows of the evil one. Take the helmet of salvation and the sword of the Spirit—which is the word of God. (Eph. 6:10–17)

The armor of God is our only defense against the flaming offense of Satan. But notice something unique about each piece of armor. Notice how each piece represents not a work of ours, but a work of God's:

- The armor is the "armor of God" (v. 13).
- The belt is God's truth (v. 14a).
- The righteousness that can protect us is God's (v. 14b).
- The sandals are the efficacy of the good news of Jesus (v. 15).
- The shield is the faith God has gifted to us (v. 16).
- The helmet is our salvation (v. 17a).
- The sword is God's Word (v. 17b).

None of these things originate in us or are anything we can do. From head to toe, we are shod in the powerful work of God. This is why Paul begins this treatise on spiritual warfare with the admonition to "be strengthened by the Lord and by *his* vast strength" (emphasis added).

The righteousness that will guard us from the accusations and devastations of the evil one is the righteousness that is credited to us by faith, bestowed to us by grace, and originates not in us but in God, who has sent his Son to become our works. The holiness we lay hold of in the gospel is the holiness that silences the serpent. Our goals, then, are to keep our eyes on the gospel of the glory of

Christ, to keep meditating on his grace, and to keep reapplying the perfect righteousness that is already ours by faith (Phil. 3:12, 16).

Good news! God helps those who cannot help themselves. God helps those who despair of their own puny attempts at salvation and turn to him for rescue. "For since he himself has suffered when he was tempted, he is able to help those who are tempted" (Heb. 2:18).

In this sense, to help yourself is to endanger yourself. In our own strength, we are sitting ducks for the devil's gnarled teeth. "Each person is tempted when he is drawn away and enticed by his own evil desire" (James 1:14). The only way to avoid being drawn away is to draw near to the only one who can save you.

GOD HELPS THOSE WHO DESPAIR OF THEMSELVES

No temptation has come upon you except what is common to humanity. But God is faithful; he will not allow you to be tempted beyond what you are able, but with the temptation he will also provide a way out so that you may be able to bear it. (1 Cor. 10:13)

What is the way out?

Satan wants you to think it's taking your salvation into your own hands. As I said in the opening to this chapter, the despair uneasily dormant in my soul is tied to this idea. But if I am my only hope, my condition is hopeless. Taking matters into my own hands was the way out of the garden!

The way out of the cursed exile is Christ himself.

So come needy. Come empty-handed. Turn out your pockets. Beat your chest, if you have to, and tear your clothes. Scrape the boils off your skin, if that's what you need to do. But whatever you do, do not come to the fruit of Christ's righteousness seeking a bargain. Do not barter, do not buy, but beg.

The blessing is for those who are poor in spirit, not rich. If you will bring the empty hand of faith, however trembling, to the infinitely holy Lord of the universe, he will fill it with the immeasurable riches of himself. There is no other way. God is actively looking to save those who cannot save themselves.

And this is good news, because it means literally anyone can qualify, provided they will get low enough. Provided we despair of ourselves, we will find his grace instantly for the having.

I think a lot about that hellish file. It contains the devil's knowledge of my weakness to temptation. I suppose it recounts all my sins, too, and all my sinful appraisals of my good works. I suppose even the devil knows that this legalist must be saved not just from his own sins but from his own righteousness. He certainly accuses me enough about it.

I think about Nealofer the Uber driver, who really believes his goodness will be good enough. I think how much more insecure I would be if I were relying on my own. Nealofer imagines that he will stand before a holy God at the end of days and his good will outweigh his bad. He envisions receiving his just reward and it *not* being eternal damnation.

Not so me. I keep an email folder on my laptop labeled "Pick-Me-Ups." When I get an especially encouraging email from someone, I file it there. Sometimes when I'm feeling down, I peruse all the messages in that file. "See?" I say to myself. "I'm a good person. People like me. I do things that matter."

I don't think I'll get to take a single one of these emails to heaven with me.

There was a CCM song in the late eighties about a guy who died and went to heaven, always wondering if what he did mattered on earth, and when he got there, he encountered a long line of people he had helped just waiting to say thank you. Our youth group used to perform it as a dramatic skit. It was super cheesy. It was also super unbiblical.

I do think we'll know our believing loved ones in heaven. I guess we'll hear thank you from them (and they from us). But the idea that our heavenly reward consists of congratulations for a life lived benevolently is not anywhere close to scriptural.

I tell you what: we better show up empty-handed, simply clinging to the cross.

Does that make you feel insecure? If it does, you are listening to lies. Do not buy the lie that God helps those who help themselves. God will utterly save those who are utterly helpless.

I want to share with you some other words from my friend Ray. I hope they will be as big an encouragement to you as they are to me.

This is our ultimate accountability. Let's get ready. Let's live with purpose. Let's live in repentance. Let's be aware, moment by moment, that right now counts forever. What we think, what we say, what we feel, what we do and don't do—we matter. We matter to Christ. We will matter forever. And very soon we will "report in." This is solemnizing. This is dignifying. It is also encouraging.

What if, as you stand there before Christ your Judge on that great and final day, surrounded by all the redeemed, each one awaiting his or her moment before the Lord—what if, standing there before him, he asks, "Everyone, I want to know who among you appreciated this person's ministry? Who would like to bear witness to how he helped you for my sake?" And no one says anything. Total silence. Awkward silence. Everyone is embarrassed. Everyone is thinking, *Would somebody please say something?* You are standing there wondering, *So my entire life comes down to this? What a failure I am!* But then one voice does break that terrible silence. The Lord himself stands and says, "Well, *I* appreciated his ministry!"

It's an improbable scenario. But putting it like that does isolate the most urgent question of all. Is the approval of Jesus enough for you and for me? Do we love him enough, do we revere him enough, that his judgment is the one we're living for?

We care what others think. We want to please them (1 Cor. 10:33). *But only one opinion will count finally and forever.*[5]

And if I could add one more thing to what Ray has said here, it would be this: The devil has a file on us, to be sure. But the Lord's got one too (Rev. 21:27).

THE AUTOPSY OF A LIE

It is written . . .

—THE SAVIOR

AFTER THE LIE, THERE WAS DEATH.

The world became a wasteland of fulfillment deterred, beauty shrouded, enlightenment stifled. The world is an amazing place, but think of the wonders if there were no curse.

When the exile of mankind from the garden began, the serpent went on to plan his dominion. Gaining more and more power over fallen men, he lay hellish claim over air (Eph. 2:2), land (Job 1:7), and sea (Rev. 12:12). Perhaps he mistakes the brokenness of creation as evidence of his own sovereignty rather than his Maker's.

The power has gone to his head. Every day with billions of men and women, his army of devils rehearses the temptation of Adam and Eve with devastating results. Maybe he thinks he can actually win.

When the Reformer Martin Luther wrote his hymn "A Mighty Fortress," one of the masterpieces of hymnody enduring to this day, he passed on to his theological descendants the stewardship to a mystery. We sing about the devil:

> For, lo, his doom is sure.
> One little word shall fell him.

I wondered for a long time, "What word is Luther talking about?" What's the "little word" that spells the devil's doom and "fell[s] him"?

It begins almost immediately after man and woman have fallen to *him*.

So the LORD God said to the serpent:

> Because you have done this,
> you are cursed more than any livestock
> and more than any wild animal.
> You will move on your belly
> and eat dust all the days of your life.
> I will put hostility between you and the woman,
> and between your offspring and her offspring.
> He will strike your head,
> and you will strike his heel.

(GEN. 3:14–15)

He is cursed too. We'll come back to that latter part, the whole thing about the crushing, because it's important. For now we note that after the fall of man, the devil's rise and defeat run together through world history.

It must gall him that he must ask for God's permission to afflict Job. He must have enjoyed hurting a righteous man, but feeling God's collar around his neck must have enraged him.

Even as the devil builds his crooked kingdom and marshals his evil troops, surely he knows it's all for naught. As he's capitalizing on men's fears and lusts, enticing their flesh, and persecuting their spirits—as he revels in the lostness of the lost and the damnation that results from it—he must know in the back of his mind that the end is nigh.

Day by day, as he helps men build monuments to themselves and thus to him, the curse has to eat away at him. And the promise too. "I will put hostility between . . . your offspring and her offspring. He will strike your head, and you will strike his heel."[1]

When he gets wind that something has changed in the world, he seethes with fear-fueled rage. He sorts out that his Maker has actually entered the atmosphere again, miraculously conceived in a virgin's womb.

The devil cannot wait to destroy the child. But he is forbidden. The baby is mightier than he. Still, he is relentless. He nips at the child's heels, and then the man's, taunting at what will be the place of his crushing.

The man goes into the wilderness. He takes the mode of the exiled sinner, perhaps even an expiated scapegoat. He has no sin himself—and this is an endless fuel of wrath for the devil—but he carries the weight of the sin of his people.

Finally he looks isolated. He looks weak. He looks a bit like Adam and Eve when they became vulnerable in that garden. He is starving and nearing the end of his human capacity for endurance.

The devil thinks, *This is my chance.*

The serpent goes to work again. This time he is more bold.

He does not disguise his propositions as questions, as he started with Eve. He practically orders his Master around!

> Then the tempter approached him and said, "If you are the Son of God, tell these stones to become bread."
>
> He answered, "It is written: Man must not live on bread alone but on every word that comes from the mouth of God."
>
> Then the devil took him to the holy city, had him stand on the pinnacle of the temple, and said to him, "If you are the Son of God, throw yourself down. For it is written:
>
> > He will give his angels orders concerning you,
> > and they will support you with their hands
> > so that you will not strike
> > your foot against a stone."
>
> Jesus told him, "It is also written: Do not test the Lord your God."
>
> Again, the devil took him to a very high mountain and showed him all the kingdoms of the world and their splendor. And he said to him, "I will give you all these things if you will fall down and worship me."
>
> Then Jesus told him, "Go away, Satan! For it is written: Worship the Lord your God, and serve only him."
>
> Then the devil left him, and angels came and began to serve him.
>
> (MATT. 4:3–11)

We can notice a few key things about the desert temptation of Jesus. First, the symmetry between the threefold temptation of

Christ and the threefold appeal of the fruit to Eve is remarkable. We see the implications for our own daily temptations in the echo of both found in 1 John 2:16, where the apostle warns, "For everything in the world—the lust of the flesh, the lust of the eyes, and the pride in one's possessions—is not from the Father, but is from the world." Note the correlations in the table below:

GENESIS 3	MATTHEW 4	1 JOHN 2	PROMISE
Good for food	Stone to bread	Lust of the flesh	Fulfillment
Delight to the eyes	Splendor of the kingdoms	Lust of the eyes	Beauty
Will make wise	Angelic enthronement	Pride in possessions	Enlightenment

Second, as we've mentioned before, Jesus resists the devil where Adam and Eve did not. We see how in both temptations, the question of God's Word comes up. The devil wants to start his own Bible study, and all his insights begin with the phrase "To me, this means . . ."

Eve was lulled to spiritual sleep by this subtle refrain. Jesus, despite his extreme fatigue, is not. At every point where Satan effectively says, "Did God really say . . . ?," Jesus counters with an "It is written."

Our deliverance began at the incarnation and was officially inaugurated at Christ's baptism, but here in the desert is where it begins to take doctrinal shape before our eyes. We are meant to see the clear contrast between the disobedience of Adam and the obedience of Christ. And while Adam's disobedience became ours, we are meant to see in the temptation of Jesus that the Second Adam's obedience can become ours too.

Where our death began in a garden, our life began in the wilderness. From this moment on, things appear to move more quickly. Even the Son of Man's friends begin to exercise authority over demonic powers. They marvel at this, and Jesus says, "I watched Satan fall from heaven like lightning" (Luke 10:18).

The kingdom of God is underway in the ministry of Christ, and the kingdom of Satan is beginning to crumble. All the devil's tenuous domain is being reclaimed. Like the children of Israel plundering the Philistine camp after David defeated the unbeatable Goliath, Christ's disciples, through his blossoming victory, are kicking butt and taking names.

In response to being called the devil, Jesus rebukes the blasphemy and says, "But no one can enter a strong man's house and plunder his possessions unless he first ties up the strong man. Then he can plunder his house" (Mark 3:27).

Jesus is saying, in other words, that not only is he not the devil but he has come to defeat the devil and take back all that was stolen. It is the foreshadow of more to come (Rev. 20:2).

In the meantime, the devil has become more frantic. His lies have become more outrageous. But he is just as crafty as ever at wooing us with them.

The gospel according to Satan doesn't sound like you think it would. As Donald Barnhouse once suggested, if the devil took over a city, it wouldn't be glutted with bars and porn shops and pool halls; instead, it would be full of well-mannered, tidy pedestrians who were all polite and nice and filled churches where Christ isn't preached. The devil knows he doesn't need the Church of Satan to get you. He just needs something shiny. He comes to us, remember, as an angel of light (2 Cor. 11:14). He makes, as Paul called them, "arguments that sound reasonable" (Col. 2:4).

We have examined eight lies throughout this book. But they don't sound exactly like lies, do they? The devil makes his lies sound like common wisdom, religious insight, or motivational speeches.

Maybe you wish I'd said more about the devil himself in this book, more about demons and so-called spiritual warfare. But we've been doing spiritual warfare all along. Nothing is gained through an obsessive focus on the devil. So I have largely put the figure of Satan in the background, in part to avoid one of the errors Lewis mentioned in his preface to *The Screwtape Letters*:

> There are two equal and opposite errors into which our race can fall about the devils. One is to disbelieve in their existence. The other is to believe, and to feel an excessive and unhealthy interest in them. They themselves are equally pleased by both errors and hail a materialist or a magician with the same delight.[2]

No, I am convinced the best way to stay alert is to focus not so much on the devil's being but on his *doing*. And in learning how to apply the work of Christ to our resisting of satanic influence, we must look at what Christ was doing too.

IT IS WRITTEN

The Christian must combat hellish lies with heavenly truths. The antidote for worldly wisdom isn't more of the same, but the wisdom that comes from on high. This means that every Christian must be a person of biblical doctrine. We will notice the crafty, plausible reasoning of the devil's lies only if we are well-studied in the solid, godly declarations of God's Word.

In Ephesians 4, Paul begins extrapolating precious truths for Christian strength from the doctrines of the divine Trinity and the bodily ascension of Jesus. Then he makes a direct connection between these doctrinal truths and our ability to withstand lies: "Then we will no longer be little children, tossed by the waves and blown around by every wind of teaching, by human cunning with cleverness in the techniques of deceit" (v. 14).

If you are theologically flimsy when the devil shows up, you are ripe for his picking. You may even want to chart out ways that key Christian doctrines can help guard against particular weaknesses commonly exploited by Satan. Consider something like the chart below:

VULNERABILITY	DOCTRINE
Doubt/Insecurity	Perseverance of the Saints
Fear	The Spirit's Indwelling
Timidity	The Fruit of the Spirit
Guilt	Expiation
Condemnation	Propitiation
Fear of Death	The Resurrection and Ascension
Fear of the Future	Progressive Sanctification and the Second Coming of Christ
Distrust of God	The Inerrancy and Historicity of Scripture
Legalism	Grace

| Loneliness | Ecclesiology (Theology of the Church) |
| Pride | Hamartiology (Doctrine of Sin) |

Your list could be longer and more detailed, but you get the idea.

Remember that you don't have to be an academic scholar to fulfill the mandate to combat weakness with doctrinal truth. But at the very least every Christian must be a student of God's Word. We cannot spot the counterfeits of Satan if we are not fluent in the truths of God.

We see how Christ's defense against the devil's lies began at each point with the phrase "It is written." This must be our defense as well.

When the devil comes to accuse us, we say, "It is written [in Job 16:19], 'Even now my witness is in heaven, and my advocate is in the heights!'" We say, "It is written [in 1 John 2:1], 'if anyone does sin, we have an advocate with the Father—Jesus Christ the righteous one.'"

When the devil comes to weaken us, we say, "It is written [in Eph. 6:10], 'Finally, be strengthened by the Lord and by his vast strength.'"

When the devil comes to diminish the cross before our eyes, we say, "It is written [in 1 Cor. 2:2], 'I decided to know nothing among you except Jesus Christ and him crucified.'"

When the devil comes to make us doubt our faith, we say, "It is written [in 2 Thess. 3:3], 'But the Lord is faithful; he will strengthen and guard [me] from the evil one.'"

At every point of satanic attack, we can have a word of Spirit-breathed truth at our disposal. For every one of his "Did God really say . . . ?" insinuations, we have an arsenal of "It is written" declarations.

The devil comes to steal, kill, and destroy, and we are thoroughly equipped by God's Word (2 Tim. 3:16–17) to rebuke him, for he cannot steal what we know is ours in Christ, he cannot kill what has been united to Christ, and he cannot destroy what has been eternally safeguarded in Christ. When he comes in a million different ways, with lies big and little, subtle and unsubtle, to condemn us in the face of all grace, we say to him, "Be gone, devil. For it is written, there is no condemnation for those who are in Christ" (Rom. 8:1).

Our enemy is shrewd, so it would be shrewder still of you to take as much of the Bible to heart as you can to be prepared for his schemes. That last verse in particular begins a chapter that might be a mighty good place to start. Romans 8 is a treasure chest of Christian promises and an armory of heavenly defenses.

Consider how some precious truths of Romans 8 help us even as we confront the shiny lies we've covered in this book:

LIE	ESSENTIAL PROBLEM(S)	ANTIDOTE FROM ROMANS 8
"God just wants you to be happy."	Making pleasure ultimate	Romans 8:5–6
"You only live once."	Taking no thought of your soul	Romans 8:12–13
"You just need to live your truth."	Self-centeredness/ Faithlessness	Romans 8:14–17
"What you feel is reality."	Hopelessness, despair	Romans 8:18, 24–28, 38–39

"This world is what you make it."	Pride/Idolatry of self	Romans 8:19–23, 29–30
"You need to let go and let God."	Antinomianism	Romans 8:2–4, 37
"The cross is not about wrath."	Condemnation	Romans 8:1, 31–39
"God helps those who help themselves."	Legalism	Romans 8:15

The true gospel promises of Romans 8, and many other Scripture passages besides, are the antidote to the false gospel of the devil.

But we must remember that even the devil will use Scripture to his own ends. If he can twist them so that we take our eyes off the glory of God, he'll quote Bible verses all the livelong day. What he doesn't want is for our gaze to trace the truths of Scripture to the radiance of God's glory (Heb. 1:3), who is Christ Jesus the Redeemer.

So now that we've seen the anatomy of the lie, let's perform its autopsy.

IT. IS. FINISHED.

Before Christ breathed his last on the cross, he did not cry out, "It has begun," though of course many things were beginning through his death. He did not cry out, "It is possible," as if his death created a hypothetical spirituality, an open-ended victory that further depends on the strength of its believers. No, he cried out, "It is finished" (John 19:30).

The mission was always to suffer and die, and the spiritual turnabout was cataclysmic. For in receiving the penalty for our sins on the cross, Jesus also through his death ransoms slaves from their bondage to sin and evil, performs justice in the light of God's righteousness, and conquers the powers of wickedness (Col. 2:15).

Like Haman on his own gallows (Est. 7:10), the devil's hope for Christ's cross becomes his own undoing.

> Now since the children have flesh and blood in common, Jesus also shared in these, so that through his death he might destroy the one holding the power of death—that is, the devil—and free those who were held in slavery all their lives by the fear of death. (Heb. 2:14–15)

In his resurrection, he conquers even the last enemy, death itself (1 Cor. 15:26), and swallows it up forever. Jesus' resurrection signals that life for him and his siblings goes on forever, but the devil's days are numbered.

These are things the devil doesn't want you to know. If you're going to be in the Bible, he wants you looking out of a self-interested and Christ-deficient moralism. He wants you to read the law as a means of self-righteousness and judgmentalism. He wants you to read wrath as if it is the final word and grace as if it costs you something.

From now on, you and I must always read "It is written" in the light of "It is finished."

How fast and loose the devil is with Scripture! In his temptation of Jesus to throw himself off the temple, the devil quotes Psalm 91:11–12, but he stops short of verse 13. Why? Because it says that the same foot supported by the angels will "trample on the serpent."

And thus we come full circle.

In the curse we are told that Adam's offspring will have their heels struck by the serpent, whose head will be crushed by the same (Gen. 3:15). Sure enough, just as foreshadowed, the Second Adam, Jesus the Christ, has his heel struck by the serpent. But despite the nail through his feet—indeed, because of it!—he has crushed the serpent's head.

When we put our faith in Jesus, his righteous victory becomes ours too. As Paul wrote in Romans 16:20, "The God of peace will soon crush Satan under *your* feet" (emphasis added).

The apostle John said, "The Son of God was revealed for this purpose: to destroy the devil's works" (1 John 3:8). And he will not stop until he is done. In Revelation 20:7–10 we see the final act in Christ's conquest of evil for his glory and our good:

> When the thousand years are completed, Satan will be released from his prison and will go out to deceive the nations at the four corners of the earth, Gog and Magog, to gather them for battle. Their number is like the sand of the sea. They came up across the breadth of the earth and surrounded the encampment of the saints, the beloved city. Then fire came down from heaven and consumed them. The devil who deceived them was thrown into the lake of fire and sulfur where the beast and the false prophet are, and they will be tormented day and night forever and ever.

You know where liars go. And those who persist in believing the devil's lies about God and grace will go there too. Hell is just as real as the devil himself. And this match is made in heaven, from which Christ himself came to obey perfectly on our behalf, die sacrificially as our substitute, rise triumphantly as our eternal life, and ascend gloriously to prepare our home, where we will be with him when he returns.

The good news is that because of he who is the Truth, sinners can go to heaven, and the devil can go to hell.

ACKNOWLEDGMENTS

IT IS NO LIE THAT EVERY BOOK I'VE WRITTEN HAS sprung from an imagination well served by friends and colleagues who have encouraged and ministered to me in ways incalculable. I am especially grateful for support from:

- the pastors at Liberty Baptist Church;
- my students and co-laborers at Spurgeon College and Midwestern Seminary;
- my indefatigable agent, Don Gates;
- the stellar editorial team at Thomas Nelson, including literary sherpa Webster Younce.

And, as always, I am forever indebted to Becky, Macy, and Grace, who laugh easily, love patiently, and endure graciously. I'll buy y'all something nice when the check comes in. I love you.

NOTES

INTRODUCTION

1. Frederick S. Leahy, *Satan Cast Out: A Study in Biblical Demonology* (Edinburgh, UK: Banner of Truth, 2017), 35.
2. Mike McKinley, *Did the Devil Make Me Do It? And Other Questions About Satan, Demons and Evil Spirits* (Epsom, UK: Good Book Company, 2013), 64–65.
3. Thomas Brooks, *Precious Remedies Against Satan's Devices* (Edinburgh, UK: Banner of Truth, 1997), 230.

CHAPTER 1: GOD JUST WANTS YOU TO BE HAPPY

1. Leonardo Blair, "Victoria Osteen Ripped for Telling Church 'Just Do Good For Your Own Self'; Worship Is Not for God, 'You're Doing It for Yourself,'" *The Christian Post*, August 30, 2014, https://www.christianpost.com/news/victoria-osteen-ripped-for-telling-church-just-do-good-for-your-own-self-worship-is-not-for-god-youre-doing-it-for-yourself.html.
2. George Whitefield, "Walking with God" in *Selected Sermons of George Whitefield*, Christian Classics Ethereal Library, http://www.ccel.org/ccel/whitefield/sermons.iv.html.
3. Ligon Duncan, "Victoria Osteen, the Glory of God and Reformed Worship," LigonDuncan.com, September 1, 2014, https://ligonduncan.com/victoria-osteen-the-glory-of-god-and-reformed-worship/.

4. David Prince, "In Defense of Christian Happiness," For The Church, November 25, 2015, https://ftc.co/resource-library/blog -entries/in-defense-of-christian-happiness.

5. Prince, "In Defense of Christian Happiness."

6. Lewis, *The Screwtape Letters*, 38–39.

CHAPTER 2: YOU ONLY LIVE ONCE

1. Matthew McCullough, *Remember Death: The Surprising Path to Living Hope* (Wheaton, IL: Crossway, 2018), 19–22.

2. McCullough, *Remember Death*, 155.

3. John Piper, *Seeing and Savoring Jesus Christ* (Wheaton, IL: Crossway, 2004), 72.

4. C. S. Lewis, *Till We Have Faces* (New York: Harcourt, 1957), 279.

CHAPTER 3: YOU NEED TO LIVE YOUR TRUTH

1. Dietrich Bonhoeffer, *Creation and Fall/Temptation: Two Biblical Studies* (New York: Collier, 1959), 73.

2. See Romans 12:19; Matthew 6:15.

3. Joe Heim, "Jerry Falwell Jr. Can't Imagine Trump 'Doing Anything That's Not Good for the Country,'" *Washington Post*, January 1, 2019, https://www.washingtonpost.com/lifestyle /magazine/jerry-falwell-jr-cant-imagine-trump-doing-anything -thats-not-good-for-the-country/2018/12/21/6affc4c4-f19e-11e8 -80d0-f7e1948d55f4_story.html.

4. Rod Dreher, "The Ben Carson Option," *The American Conservative*, October 14, 2016, https://www.theamericanconservative.com /dreher/the-ben-carson-option/.

5. Milton, *Paradise Lost*, 91.

6. Gilbert K. Chesterton, *Orthodoxy* (New York: John Lane, 1909), 135–36.

7. Jackie Hill Perry (@jackhillperry), "Since God is holy and utterly good by nature, even His harshest commands are worth your obedience," Twitter, January 2, 2019, 10:14 a.m., https://twitter .com/jackiehillperry/status/1080497637277794304?s=21.

CHAPTER 4: YOUR FEELINGS ARE REALITY

1. Bessel van der Kolk, *The Body Keeps the Score: Brain, Mind, and Body in the Healing of Trauma* (New York: Penguin, 2015), 44–45.
2. Van der Kolk, *Body Keeps the Score*, 275.
3. In reply to Charles Hugo, quoted in *The Congregationalist* 77 (November 10, 1892), 420.
4. George Herbert, "The Collar," in *George Herbert: The Complete English Works* (New York: Alfred Knopf, 1995), 149–150.
5. J. R. R. Tolkien, *The Return of the King* (Boston: Houghton Mifflin, 1965), 344.
6. C. S. Lewis, *The Great Divorce* (New York: Macmillan, 1975), 67.
7. Susan M. Shaw, *God Speaks to Us, Too: Southern Baptist Women on Church, Home, and Society* (Lexington, KY: University Press of Kentucky, 2008), 217.
8. George Whitefield, "The Folly and Danger of Parting with Christ for the Pleasures and Profits of Life," in *The Sermons of George Whitefield*, vol. 1, ed. Lee Gattis (Wheaton, IL: Crossway, 2012), 375.

CHAPTER 5: YOUR LIFE IS WHAT YOU MAKE IT

1. Peter Sblendorio, "Kylie Jenner Is Worth $900 Million and On Pace to Become Youngest Self-Made Billionaire Ever," *New York Daily News*, July 11, 2018, https://www.nydailynews.com /entertainment/ny-ent-kylie-jenner-worth-900-million-20180711 -story.html.
2. April Salud, "Watch Jim Carrey's Hilarious and Poignant Interview for 'Jim & Andy: The Great Beyond,'" *The Hollywood Reporter*, September 11, 2017, https://www.hollywoodreporter.com/news /toronto-watch-jim-carreys-hilarious-poignant-interview-jim-andy -great-beyond-1037794.
3. Richard Baxter, *Dying Thoughts* (Edinburgh, UK: Banner of Truth, 2009), 35.
4. Oscar Wilde, "Ye Shall Be Gods," in *The Complete Works of Oscar Wilde: Volume 1*, edited by Bobby Fong and Karl Beckson (Oxford, UK: Oxford University Press, 2000), 1.

5. William Ernest Henley, *Echoes of Life and Death: Forty-Seven Lyrics* (Portland, ME: Thomas B. Mosher, 1908), 7.

6. Dietrich Bonhoeffer, *Creation and Fall / Temptation: Two Biblical Studies* (New York: Collier, 1959), 77.

CHAPTER 6: YOU NEED TO LET GO AND LET GOD

1. J. I. Packer, Introduction to John Owen's *On the Mortification of Sin*, 10.

2. Andy Naselli, *No Quick Fix: Where Higher Life Theology Came From, What It Is, and Why It's Harmful* (Bellingham, WA: Lexham Press, 2017), 48.

3. Trevin Wax, "Wake Me Up, Lord!: A Review of Jared Wilson's 'Gospel Wakefulness,'" Kingdom People blog, The Gospel Coalition, October 12, 2011, https://www.thegospelcoalition.org /blogs/trevin-wax/wake-me-up-lord-a-review-of-jared-wilsons -gospel-wakefulness/.

4. Jared C. Wilson, *Gospel Wakefulness* (Wheaton, IL: Crossway, 2011), 27–28.

5. Andy Naselli, *No Quick Fix: Where Higher Life Theology Came From, What It Is, and Why It's Harmful* (Bellingham, WA: Lexham Press, 2017), 52–53.

6. W. H. Griffith Thomas, "The Victorious Life (I.)," *Bibliotheca Sacra* 76 (1919), 275, quoted in Naselli, *No Quick Fix*, 30.

7. I say more about the wrongheadedness of the idea of "letting God" in chapter 5 (on prayer) in my book *Supernatural Power for Everyday People: Experiencing God's Extraordinary Spirit in Your Ordinary Life* (Nashville: Nelson, 2018).

8. Dallas Willard, *The Great Omission: Reclaiming Jesus's Essential Teachings on Discipleship* (New York: HarperCollins, 2006), 166.

9. R. C. Sproul, "Should I 'Let Go and Let God'?," interview by Nathan W. Bingham, *Ligonier*, June 27, 2018, https://www .ligonier.org/blog/should-i-let-go-and-let-god/.

CHAPTER 7: THE CROSS IS NOT ABOUT WRATH

1. All of these ideas are listed in the table of contents in William Paul Young, *Lies We Believe About God* (New York: Atria, 2017), ix–x.
2. William Paul Young, *Lies We Believe About God* (New York: Atria, 2017), 150–51.
3. Young, *Lies We Believe About God*, 169.
4. I shared a shorter paraphrase of this encounter in my book *The Gospel-Driven Church: Uniting Church Growth Dreams with the Metrics of Grace* (Grand Rapids, MI: Zondervan, 2019), 132–33.
5. Jared C. Wilson, *Gospel Deeps: Reveling in the Excellencies of Jesus* (Wheaton, IL: Crossway, 2012).
6. Steve Jeffery, Michael Ovey, and Andrew Sach, *Pierced for Our Transgressions: Rediscovering the Glory of Penal Substitution* (Wheaton, IL: Crossway, 2007), 230.
7. Derek Rishmawy, "The Beauty of the Cross: 19 Objections and Answers on Penal Substitutionary Atonement (500th Post)," *Reformedish*, October 23, 2014, https://derekzrishmawy.com /2014/10/23/the-beauty-of-the-cross-19-objections-and-answers-on -penal-substitutionary-atonement-500th-post/.
8. Timothy George, "No Squishy Love," *First Things*, July 29, 2013, https://www.firstthings.com/web-exclusives/2013/07/no-squishy -love.
9. Michael Vlach, "Penal Substitution in Church History," *The Master's Seminary Journal* (Fall 2009), 199–214. See also chapter 5 on "Surveying the Heritage: The Historical Pedigree of Penal Substitution" in Jeffery, Ovey, and Sach, *Pierced for Our Transgressions*, 161–204.
10. William Paul Young, *Lies We Believe About God* (New York: Atria, 2017), 151.
11. Mark Dever and Michael Lawrence, *It Is Well: Expositions on Substitutionary Atonement* (Wheaton, IL: Crossway, 2010), 124.
12. J. I. Packer, "What Did the Cross Achieve?: The Logic of Penal Substitution," in J. I. Packer and Mark Dever, *In My Place*

Condemned He Stood: Celebrating the Glory of the Atonement (Wheaton, IL: Crossway, 2007), 79.

13. Packer, *In My Place*, 77.

14. I am indebted to Tim Keller for his April 5, 2017, message at The Gospel Coalition National Conference; "Boasting in Nothing Except the Cross" (a sermon on Galatians 6) featured this concluding anecdote. Keller himself credited the story to (and quotes) Dick Lucas. I have largely paraphrased Keller's version of events but re-created his dialogue as accurately as I was able. You can watch or listen to the sermon at the TGC website via the following link: https://www.thegospelcoalition.org/conference _media/boasting-nothing-except-cross/.

CHAPTER 8: GOD HELPS THOSE WHO HELP THEMSELVES

1. Cited in Albert Mohler, "The Scandal of Biblical Illiteracy: It's Our Problem," Albert Mohler blog, January 20, 2016, https: //albertmohler.com/2016/01/20/the-scandal-of-biblical-illiteracy -its-our-problem-4/.

2. "Competing Worldviews Influence Today's Christians," Barna Group, May 9, 2017, https://www.barna.com/research/competing -worldviews-influence-todays-christians/.

3. Moroni 10:32, The Book of Mormon, https://www.lds.org /scriptures/bofm/moro/10.32.

4. 2 Nephi 25:23, The Book of Mormon, https://www.lds.org /scriptures/bofm/2-ne/25.23.

5. Ray Ortlund, "Right Now Counts Forever," The Gospel Coalition, December 19, 2018, https://www.thegospelcoalition.org/blogs /ray-ortlund/right-now-counts-forever/.

CONCLUSION

1. Genesis 3:15.

2. Lewis, *The Screwtape Letters*, 7.

ABOUT THE AUTHOR

JARED C. WILSON is assistant professor of pastoral ministry at Spurgeon College, author in residence at Midwestern Seminary, general editor of For The Church (ftc.co), and director of the Pastoral Training Center at Liberty Baptist Church in Kansas City, Missouri. He is the award-winning author of numerous books, including *Supernatural Power for Everyday People*, *The Imperfect Disciple*, and *The Gospel-Driven Church*. Jared blogs regularly at For The Church, where he also hosts the *For The Church* podcast, and at The Gospel Coalition, and he speaks at numerous churches and conferences around the world every year. He lives outside Kansas City with his wife, Becky, and their two daughters.

You can visit Jared online at jaredcwilson.com.